The *Fairly* Truthful Guide to Geordie

A humorous celebration of
a unique region and its language

Written, compiled and illustrated by
Gary Hogg

Illustrations ©Gary Hogg
Quiz photographs ©Chris Tweedy
Original cover photograph ©CMT.Harrison

First published in Great Britain 2007

British Library Cataloguing in Publication Data.
A catalogue record for this book is available
from the British Library

ISBN 978-0-9544794-2-8

Published by Toontoons
42 Dunkeld Close
Blyth
NE24 3SP

Printed in China by
1010 Printing International Limited

Design by Ian Scott Design

Website: www.garyhogg.co.uk

Contents

Dedicated to my mam
Marion Burryman Hogg
1916 - 2007

Acknowledgements

Grateful thanks to family and friends for their support through the years
and their help in providing material for this book.

Bernard Wrigley, Brian McGuire, Chris & Keith Hartnell,
Colin Pearson, Fred Burke, Fred Hogg, Jess & Dave,
Johnny Handle, Karis Jones, Lucy & Guy Falkenau,
Malcolm Collins, Neil Atkinson, Ray Hooker, Bill Maynard
Sandra Hogg, Tom McConville,
and the Herg family from Aallower.

Carol Davison for checking out my recipes and
making sure no one gets poisoned.

Chris Tweedy for the quiz photographs – visit his website for a
variety of views of Newcastle and the surrounding area.
www.monkchester.co.uk

Chris Harrison for the photograph from which the
cover image was produced. Visit his website to
see the original and many others.
www.newcastleupontynedailyphoto.com

The Fairly Truthful Guide To Geordie

We all know that light travels faster than sound. This would explain why some people appear quite bright until they open their mouths.

Upon first hearing a person's voice, we are all guilty of putting them into a social slot. We jump to conclusions as to their educational, financial and even emotional standing. The North East of England has for many years suffered adversely from this custom. The Geordie dialect is often perceived as an improper use of English. However, whilst the rest of the country adopted the English language, centuries of geographic and social isolation resulted in Geordies having little outside influence on a language given to them in Anglo-Saxon times.

Although long gone are the stereotypical cloth caps, whippets, dole queues and Woodbines, this is the heritage from which we still derive most of our humour. The average Geordie now lives comfortably, works for a living and is just as likely to drink a glass of Cabernet Sauvignon as a pint. There is very little class distinction on Tyneside. The football ground and pubs are shared amongst students, window cleaners, retired welders and chartered accountants. You are as likely to share a quayside pint with a barrister, as you are a checkout operator.

Our ancestors were the driving force behind the industrial revolution at home and abroad. Inventions and innovations, backed by the essential coal, iron and skilled workforce, brought so much to the world. Still at the forefront, our industry has been replaced by revolutionary, scientific and medical research.

This book celebrates the rich legacy of an often-overlooked part of Britain. It's an area of beautiful coastlines and countryside with an exciting city of culture, commerce and fun, inhabited by people with a healthier than usual pride in their birthright.

About the Author

Nanna Hogg helped deliver me in the front room of number eleven, Boston Avenue, Benton Lodge. My birth certificate says within the County Borough of Newcastle upon Tyne. It was a posh new council estate isolated from the rest of the world by private houses. Our neighbours included Ministry workers from various parts of the country. Two or three well-spoken families from Yorkshire and others from further south kept spotless houses and well trimmed gardens. You know the type: they all had a lounge - we had a sitting room. 'Don't come out to the bread van wearing your apron, dear!' Mrs Tibbs told my mam one day.

Auntie Tibbs, from number twenty, was a Londoner who I thought at the time was at least upper middle-class. Her house smelled of carbolic soap. She was wealthy enough to buy a chicken for Sunday dinner and only use one drumstick and part of one breast. Then she'd wrap the remains in paper and leave it on our step. It was gratefully received and would feed our family of six for the next two or three days with stew and broth, regardless of the carbolic tinge.

My Dad, despite an upbringing in Northumberland and later Benton, chose to be a Jesmond Geordie. 'Born a gentleman but not required' Nanna Mac once said. He corrected any mis-pronunciation and bad use of grammar, even when we were toddlers.

Mam was a Lancashire lass born of Scottish parents and had lived most of her life in Carlisle. Despite spending the next sixty-odd years in the North East her accent remained a mystery.

My sister and two brothers were born in Carlisle. So my pre-school years had very little true Geordie influence. There were to be three turning points.

At the age of four and a bit I started at Benton Park Primary School and met children who spoke slightly more Geordie than those on our cloistered little estate. On our first day, Miss Lilley or it might've been Miss Thompson, asked if anyone could sing a song. Various girls got up and sang 'Baa baa black sheep' and the like. I was the only boy who was game and when asked, I sang the theme song from Rawhide complete with the entire cowboy lingo and whip cracking. I could've done Davy Crockett as an encore but wasn't encouraged. Within a few years another teacher, Norman Willey, himself a Geordie, insisted that we learned Tyneside songs. Along with the piano-thumping headmistress, Miss Green, those old gems 'Adam Buckham O' and 'Bobby Shaftoe' encouraged us to cherish our rich inheritance. I still learned the Cheyenne and Maverick theme songs in my own time though.

At a little over five years old I accompanied my father in his Ford Popular van to visit relations in Burradon and Cramlington. They worked in the pits and had offered to let us have some of their allowance of free coal. I don't know how the deal had been struck. We didn't have phones. Maybe a deal hadn't been struck. Maybe Dad just dropped in to cadge some! Burradon was probably only three miles away but the people spoke an entirely different language. I had learned to cope with the various accents of our street and the Scottish of my mam's family - and just accepted that everyone in my little corner of the world spoke differently to one another. But this was definitely foreign!

'Ye haad the perk, bonny laird. Yer da'll hoy the coals in,' said this strange man in a cap and waistcoat as he handed me a sack. My dad was able to communicate quite freely with these people presumably because he had gone to a grammar school and could also speak French quite fluently. I learned the sentence there and then so that I could tell Mam when I got back. I have never forgotten it.

My Nanna Hogg, whose forebears the McLauchlans had

escaped the Irish famine, was brought up in Ashington. She was proud of her pitmatic dialect and had a whole repertoire of Geordie sayings. Over the years many of these would filter into my everyday speech. 'Will ye tek a few soup, Hinny?' she would say when I called. I would sit on a **crackett** and tuck in. Compared with Nanna Mac's soup though, Nanna Hogg's was **nowt startlin'**.

The third defining moment in my dialectal education was to arrive the following year when the Dicksons moved in over the back. They were a lovely family, rehoused from the clearance of old terraces in the west-end of town. Mr Dickson and Uncle Jimmy worked in the shipyards and wore caps at all times. They both looked like Paw from the Broons. Mrs Dickson wore a full-length wrap-around **pinny** and headscarf and went to the shops in slippers, never mind her pinny! It was young George, aged four, who was the first to speak over the back fence.

'Wor cat's jus' gettn haad of a bord an' kilt it' was his opening line. We got talking. I told him I liked building models. 'Me da built the real HMS Hood. Wey, me Uncle Jimmy helped him like.' It was George that introduced me to words like **Coin** instead of turn, **Flannin** for flannel, **Cowped, Coyboys, Hacky** and **Bait** – an amazing vocabulary for a four year old! Remember, I had a father who would slap me for not pronouncing the ing at the end of a word and would point out every grammatical mistake that anyone in the family or indeed on the wireless dared make. I once said 'That new postman's dead like Davy Swift' to which Dad sarcastically asked 'Is Davy Swift dead?' To the Dicksons I must've sounded like Prince Charles.

Eleven-plus time came around and despite wanting to go to Manor Park School with the rest of my classmates, Dad put my name down for his old school Heaton Grammar. It was an out-of-date school that smelt of books and polish. It had a quadrangle and a tuck shop. First formers were referred to as fags, the teachers wore cloaks and corporal punishment was the norm. I received religious education from the Rev. Morton who carried one gym shoe in his briefcase for the purpose of whacking atheists and anarchists alike. I hated the school immediately. Most of my classmates were Jesmond Geordies but there were quite a few canny lads from Kenton, Heaton, Byker and Walker. Actually, most of the lads from Jesmond were canny too. We amalgamated with the girls' school when I was fourteen and that helped me through troubled times.

A wonderful form master, Dave Walker, spoke our language, called us by first names and nicknames and by getting us interested in Harry Hotspur he brightened up some some pretty tedious Shakespeare. He proved that you don't need plums in your gob to discuss literature. And he didn't show too much disappointment when years later he discovered I was fitting exhausts at a garage on Westgate Road and hadn't gone on to Cambridge. I'm sure he would've preferred to see me performing in the other West End.

At the age of seventeen I started singing in folk clubs. An early influence into the wealth of humorous Geordie songs came from Malcolm Collins - who later became Billy Fane. Malcolm, a keen analyst of the Geordie way of life, not only knew all there was to know about the works of writers Joe Wilson, Geordie Ridley and Tommy Armstrong but was also a prolific songwriter himself. His songs, about local pit closures and hardship interspersed with comical songs, ridiculed the local councils and government. He, too, was in the motor trade and we would spend as many hilarious hours welding Cortinas as we did in folk clubs.

When writing the foreword for my first book, he said 'Gary is a keen observer of life's little absurdities.' Well there's nowt more absurd than the Geordie language.

Geordieland and its Various Dialects

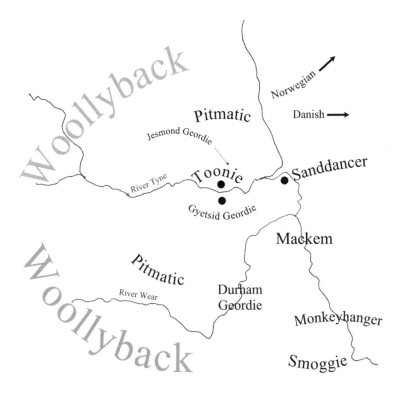

Sanddancer, an affectionate term for the canny folks of Shields, originates from a unit of Tigris bargemen employed by the Romans to move their supplies around. They were stationed at Arbeia (The place of the Arabs) which is now South Shields.

Whilst persons as far apart as Darlington and Berwick are thrilled to be referred to as Geordies, it must be noted that the indigenous tribes of the Republic of Mackemland often take it as an insult. Similarly, some citizens of Jesmond, which lies within the Toon boundaries, also wish to distance themselves from the correct use of our language.

What is a Geordie?

As Douglas Adams almost said, 'Far away in the uncharted backwaters of the once unfashionable North East of England lies an often-unregarded civilisation. Orbiting this at a distance of a few hundred miles is the rest of the British Isles. The life forms inhabiting this area are often thought of as primitive as they still think wearing warm clothing is a pretty sissy thing to do.'

The North of England is considered by many as anywhere not south of London. This would suggest that places like

Northampton and Northwich also fall into this category.

For the people of Newcastle, who have to drive south for a few hours to reach Birmingham - which is classed as up north, this is VERY confusing. And we have to travel in a southwesterly direction to reach Manchester which is classed as the North West.

So what is a Geordie? Well there are lots of different ideas on the subject, so take your pick. Earliest reports reckoned it was a name given to the people of the North East who supported the Hanoverian King George and made such a stronghold of the area that the Jacobites didn't bother pestering us too much. Now this is where it gets complicated. Why did we have a Hanoverian king in the first place? Well, when Queen Anne died, they had to find a successor who wasn't a Catholic - on account of the new Act of Settlement. Of course, the next fifty-odd in line were all Catholics. It wasn't till they got to the fifty-second in line that they found George. You would think he would have been chuffed but he wasn't. He was already a King in Germany you see. There's a limit to how much ruling a person can be bothered with.

So, reluctantly, he popped over for a visit, didn't trouble himself learning our language and decided that a government should do everything for him. A bit like today's monarch really. He invented a Prime Minister and then went swanning about doing things that didn't really matter – huntin', shootin', fishin' and maybe handing out the odd sports trophy. Actually it was quite a good setup. But most of the English people thought he was a bit of a nutter.

He was succeeded by his son. George the eleventh - I think that's probably George the second but it's spelled '11'.

By this time, the people of Northumberland and the borders, who thought he was a canny lad, were calling him Geordy or Geordie. My forty-second cousin, James Hogg, the borders poet, was one of the first to put it in writing it seems, in a song called 'Cam Ye Ower Frae France' which he wrote in the mid 1700s.

Now when it came to George the hundred and eleventh - sorry, that's probably George the third.....Well!! Now he definitely wasn't plumb. You'll have heard of him. A total **heed-the-baall**. And so, and you're not going to like this, the posh people of the city referred to the pit villagers and farming communities as Geordies and anyone who was a bit simple was referred to as a stupid Geordie. Aye, it's probably not true, any of that. It's now a more than affectionate term used throughout the country.

Others reckon it was a name given to our local pitmen who preferred using the 'Geordie' safety lamp made by George Stephenson as opposed to the Davy lamp made by er... Davy Crockett. Probably.

Then some folks say it came from the name of the collier ships which transported coals from the great north coalfields to London.

Whichever of these possibilities you choose and wherever the name comes from, it refers to the canny folk of Tyneside, Northumberland and Durham. From our borders with Yorkshire at one end to the Scottish borders at the other, most people are proud to be called Geordies. There's no particular rule although, you can't support a football team from S*nd*rl*nd. There are small pockets of these supporters who have infiltrated the Tyneside towns of Hebburn, Jarrow and South Shields and some Washington folks have been known to have Mackem tendencies. Wherever you live though, if you're proud to be called a Geordie - we're proud to have you.

History of the Geordie Language

The Geordie language has a long and interesting history, probably dating back to prehistoric times when Britain was joined to mainland Europe - and Denmark was just a long walk over the fields. Our history has been more accurately recorded since then though.

Being so far north we suffered little disturbance from the French invaders. The Romans only came as far north as Newcastle then chickened out presumably because of how cold it always is.

A fortified wall was built to mark the northernmost edge of their empire. It was almost four hundred years before the Romans went home. They no longer saw the point of being this far away from a decent climate. They were sick of their Chianti being served cold, not being able to grow their own olives and colliding with natives who drove their carts on the left. So they diddled off. They just upped-sticks and left.

The first thing that happened was the humble Northumbrian farmers started nicking bits of the wall to build shelters. Less humble locals took bigger stones to build less humble fortified houses. They needed substantial houses to keep out the marauding Pictish tribes from the north that were now getting through the holes people had made in the wall by nicking stones. This isn't strictly true as Northumberland straddles the wall and communities had built up on both sides. The Scottish border is now a lot further north. The land in between became a hostile arena for the Border Reivers. But that's another story.

Having been under the influence of the Romans and their language for so long, the locals should've been quite fluent in Italian. You would think, wouldn't you? But northerners are a stubborn lot (We're still not that keen on learning Latin.) However, we do have more Italian restaurants per person than any other city in the UK. Apart from words like **netty** derived from the Italian **cabinetti**, we still spoke the native Welsh. No, honestly. Welsh was the language. So if you think Tom Jones sometimes sounds like a Geordie, well ...it's not unusual.

The Romans had been a mighty force and without them the rich lands and towns of the North East were quite vulnerable. In an effort to protect our resources it was decided to look overseas for help. Mercenaries were brought in and, in exchange for bits of land, they swelled the ranks of our defence force and kept the Picts where they belonged. So for the next few years we were under the influence of the Anglo-Saxons ...which must've suited us because the Geordie language is the closest thing you'll get to the original Anglo Saxon.

Don't believe me? Here's some examples:
Hoose, Deed, Heed, Gan, Wrang, Alang, Strang, Nuw, Larn, and **Aad** - all Anglo Saxon words. So Gannin' alang the Scotswood Road isn't just our pronunciation it's an actual language.

You might think **gan** is from the Scottish - no, although the Scottish picked it up too. And **alang** - now people think that's just our accent but no, it's the way we were **larned** to speak. So Geordies are really using a vocabulary that has been passed down rather than one that has evolved from a poor use of the English adopted by other parts of the country.

As well as the influences from Denmark and Germany, there are lots of words that are a straight lift from Scandinavian that came with the Vikings. **Gannin' hyem** (pronounced yairm) for instance - and of course the Normans chipped in with words such as **bonny** which is derived from the French **bon**. On a Belgian website recently I noticed their 'Who's who' page was named 'Wie is Wie.'

Look at the sentence: 'The bairn's fishin for tiddlers in the born. He'll get wrang.'

Now you might think **bairn** is Scottish but the Norwegians brought it here first. The Norse word is **barn**. Another Anglo-Saxon word here **born** means stream. And this sentence:
'Is there nee shuggy boats at the **hoppins** this year?'

Hoppins - not just the biggest travelling fair in Europe that visits Newcastle every year but any fair was referred to as a **Hoppen** by guess who? The Anglo-Saxons. I don't think they'd heard of shuggy boats though. Or dunchycars.

Schools are given the task of teaching children English. Sadly, we are losing our own language. So we can sympathise with the Welsh desperately trying to hang on to their native tongue.

SAY 'WEY AYE'

19

Pronunciation

The written word is never the best way to discuss pronunciation and will never substitute for spending a year or two on Tyneside, listening. It is definitely the most recognisable but also the most difficult regional accent to master. Top class impressionists can do a good Geordie accent but they think that Jimmy Nail sounds like Kevin Whateley and Sting sounds like Alan Shearer. We can spot massive differences. Just like we can spot that the Geordie commentary on Channel Four's 'Big Brother' is a poor exaggeration.

The industrial revolution brought country folk and their parlance into the urban areas so we have various sub-categories of dialect including: the pitmatic of villages to the north of town and the outlying villages of Durham. There's the valley talk of the people along the Tyne via Crawcrook and Prudhoe into Hexhamshire. There's the distinctive Toon Geordies with the shipyard-inspired dialect from both sides of the Tyne, Jesmond-Geordies who have made the choice not to be identifiable and of course the new Geordie - which is a conglomeration of all of the above with some newly-coined Charva language thrown in. I must say the new Geordie-Charva word for a sausage roll – 'A Greggs dummy' made me laugh and confirmed that the humour is as strong as ever, even if we're slowly losing the dialect.

So here are some guidelines I have compiled as an enthusiastic observer, listener and native but by no means a scholar or researcher. There are bigger, heavier, sometimes better and sometimes more tedious books on the subject which I don't intend to compete with.

As if it's not bad enough having to learn a new vocabulary, perhaps the most difficult aspect of the Geordie language is the strange pronunciation of vowels. In particular the letter **A**. It has many forms.

First there's **A** as in **Newcastle** or **Auntie Sandra** or as in **dance to yer daddy** - that's not **darnce** mind. And Newcastle doesn't rhyme with **parcel** it rhymes with **tassle** - or at least up here it does. But hang on, we pronounce **plaster** as **plarster**. We must've kept that one in to confuse people.

Then there's the slightly more difficult **A** for an outsider which is the **A** as in **Blaydon Races** or **howway**... or indeed 'The **rain** in **Spain** stays **mainly** in the **plain**.' This is a long **A** with a hint of **E**. In fact there might even be a **Y** in the middle of the sound and a **UH** at the end if you really stretch it out - so shape your mouth into a grin like you're going to say **EE** and say the word **ate** - it should come out something like **eaayut**. A popular word for this quirk is **face** which is almost pronounced **fyeace** and in old Northumbrian was a definite **fyess**. That's what's known as a diphthong. It's where you start with one vowel and change halfway through. Actually, people from India pronounce **great** and **bait** perfectly, far better than southerners.

Then there's the long but flat **A** as in **caad, waarm** and **taalk** etc. Geordies picked this up from the Anglo Saxon words and not just through mispronouncing the English **A**. It can still be heard in Flemish, German, some Scandinavian languages and even West Indian. The actual sound is not far off the way Cockneys mispronounce their **ow** as in **braahn caah** instead of **brown cow** and some Welsh, Scouse and Smoggies drag their **A** in words like **calm, mark** and **dark**.

A good way of learning the vowel sounds is to listen to a traditional Tyneside song being sung correctly. In this first verse and chorus of Blaydon Races you have the opportunity to use all the various pronunciations of the vowel **A**.

We went to Blaydon Races, twas on the ninth of June
'ighteen hundred and sixty two on a summer's afternoon
We took the bus from Balmbra's an' she was heavy laden
Away we went alaang Collin'wood Street
That's on the road to Blaydon

Oh me lads. You shoulda seen us gannin'
Passin' the folks alaang the road just as they were stannin'
Aall the lads an' lasses there, aall wi' smilin' faces
Gannin' alaang the Scotswood Road
To see the Blaydon Races

Little Billy Fane recorded one of the best renditions of this song. Hailing from Dinnington, his natural speech has the pitmatic vocabulary and grammar peppered with the more modern Toon Geordie.

The next song, Billy Boy, features the Geordie **O** - Oh, Me Charmin' Billy Boy. There's also the very important Geordie **E** as in **ye** and the **A** as in **aall** again. The **ye** has an almost silent **Y** and is often more of a **ee**. And notice that the **A** in **have** is more comfortably pronounced as **hev**.

Where hev ee been aall the day, Billy Boy, Billy Boy?
Where hev ee been aall the day me Billy Boy?
Aa've been waalkin' aall the day wi me charmin' Nancy Grey
An' me Nancy kittled me fancy. Oh, me charmin' Billy Boy

Maybe this would be a good point for further discussion of the Geordie **E** as it is the easiest vowel to get wrong. The words **key** and **keel** in Geordie have different pronunciations of the vowel. Impressionists often trip up here. **Key, tea, me** etc are pronounced with a diphthong again so the syllable has two sounds. The mistake is made when they are pronounced **kee, tee** and **mee**. This is the pronunciation we reserve for longer words like Keel, Sweet, and street. It is also the way to spot a mackem! They only have one pronunciation of **E** so **keel** is pronounced **key-l**. A word like **here** in mackem is **heyer**. Strangely this pronunciation spreads as far as Cumberland.

Whilst we're spotting mackem misdemeanours, they only have one pronunciation for **oo**. So whereas we both pronounce **coo** with a diphthong, almost **cuw**, mackems say the words coo and cool with the same vowel sound and pronounce it **cuwel**.

Back to the **A** and **O**, a good song to illustrate the flat Geordie **A** is 'Dance To Yer Daddy.' Sometimes sung as 'Dance Ti Thy Daddy' but rarely in recent years since the Durham Geordie **thee, thou** and **thys** died out. The **O** in boat must be pronounced correctly and hearing Tyneside's Tom McConville sing the verse which includes the word 'bloater' will bring a tear of joy to many a Geordie eye. Tom was singing in New Zealand once and was approached by an exiled Geordie. He was amazed to find he'd held on to his accent for over thirty years. 'Mind, aa hev t' practise ivvery day like' he told Tom. Whilst on tour in Germany, Tom met a professor of languages from Frankfurt University. He told Tom, in the stereotypical German-English of 'Allo, 'Allo', that he had always been fascinated by the Geordie dialect and had studied it in depth. He then started speaking some rehearsed sentences and spoke Geordie like a native. His wife rolled her eyes and, in broken English, said 'He was already a Geordie when I married him!'

Come here me little Jacky
Nuw aa've smoked me baccy
Let's hev a bit o' cracky
Till the boat comes in
Dance ti yer daddy, sing ti yer mammy
Dance ti yer daddy, ti yer mammy sing
You shall hev a fishy on a little dishy
You shall hev a fishy when the boat comes in

Again the **have** is more comfortably pronounced **hev**. This is a strange rule that doesn't always apply. **Lake** is pronounced **lake** but **make** & **take** are **mek** & **tek**.

Then there's **eight** which is pronounced either with the diphthong **eaayut** or **ite** and **straight** that's pronounced **either streeayut** or **strite**. Both are totally acceptable. Obviously more cunning traps to catch out impersonators!

Sound is often pronounced **soond** but **five pounds** is more likely to be **five pund**. **Round** is more likely to be pronounced **rund** which is identical to the Norwegian **rundt**. There's a list of Norse words later in the book which may provide a few surprises.

There is a similar rule governing the words **reet** and **neet**, as used throughout the north of England into Yorkshire and Lancashire. On Tyneside, these are the only **ight** or **ite** words pronounced this way because they are not merely an accent peculiarity; they are a straight lift from the Old English **riht** and **niht**. So don't ever pronounce **sight** or **kite** as **seet** and **keet** or you'll just sound daft. In the north of Yorkshire, parts of Wearside and Weardale they do say **leyt** for **light** though.

Outsiders can sometimes be excused for not being able to speak correctly because they often don't hear correctly either. Whereas we have difficulty distinguishing between the cockney **A** and **I** when they say **tale** or **tile**, they often can't distinguish between our **A** and **E**. But don't get me started on Cockney. Have you noticed they pronounce the **L** at the end of a word as **ow**? A recent Sky Sports reporter informing us that there were still no goals at Millwall said 'It's stiow niow niow at Miowaow.' What chance do they have of learning our language when they contort the basic English so badly? Essex girl Jade Goody recently had difficulty getting Bollywood's Shilpa Shetty to understand the word **whale**. To the Indian lass's ear it sounded like **Wow**! When Shilpa eventually worked out what the word was, she said 'Ah, you mean **whale**!' and pronounced it in almost perfect Geordie.

The Geordie pronunciation of **I** is fairly normal when used in words like **divvent** or **winnet**. When the **I** is used in **kite** however, there is a hint of the wide grin needed to pronounce **ee**. So saying the word **pint** will widen the Geordie smile more than say, a southerner pronouncing it **point**. (They probably drink halves anyway.)

Then there's the case of **er** being pronounced **or**. So **her** becomes **hor**. We have a similar situation with **fir** or **fur** being pronounced **for**, likewise **dirty** is **dorty**, **infirmary** is **informary** etc. But not always - again this is a ploy to ambush imposters.

And while we're on the subject, the only people likely to call Newcastle Brown Ale 'Newky Brown' are students from out of the area. A resident of Tyneside refers to it as **Broon, Broon Dog, Dog** and sometimes **Jorney inti'space**.

Other grammatical quirks include:

The word **us**, pronounced **iz**, meaning **me**
'Get iz a Greggs Dummy'
Get me a sausage roll

The word **we** pronounced **wu** meaning **us** – sometimes **wuz**
'Get wuz a Greggs Dummy each'
Get us a sausage roll each

The word **me** meaning **my**
'Huw! Where's me Greggs Dummy?'
Excuse me, where is my sausage roll?

The word **'es** pronounced **eez** meaning **he has** or **his**
'Aal borst 'im if 'es ett me Greggs Dummy'
I'll punch him if he has eaten my sausage roll

Yuz is used as the plural of **you**
'Yuz coulda bowt yer aan Greggs Dummies'
You could have bought your own sausage rolls

The **be** in words like **before, because** and **behind** is often
replaced with **a** making **afore, a'cos** and **ahint**

In some areas **a** is pronounced **i** as in **sit** so 'At me nanna's
becomes 'It me nanna's.' **And** is pronounced **ind** and **to** is **ti** or
tiv if followed by a vowel. Similarly **e** is sometimes replaced with
i as in **ivvrythin'** and **nivver ivver**. Again, no particular rule
applies here which is why it is so difficult for a stranger to master
and easy for us to spot an interloper.

In the same way as some European languages put the verb at
the end of a sentence, we have some strange rules for construction
of sentences. Whereas the rest of the country would say 'Is John
in?' Geordies and some of our North West neighbours often say
'John in, is he?' or 'Gannin' to the toon, are you?'

Geordies like to punctuate sentences with odd words for no
particular reason - 'Aa'm gannin' to work like' 'What's he like
like?' 'I love beer me' or even 'I love you me' - and the ubiquitous
'man' as in 'I wish ye'd givower howkin' yer sneck, man' or
'Divvent give iz paste in me bait man mutha man'

The word **but** appears at the end of sentences rather than the
beginning. So the English 'But how can that be?' becomes 'How
can that be but?' so it replaces the word **though**.

'**Mind**' is another good punctuation: 'The bus is late th' day
mind.' Sometimes all three are used 'It's narf caad th' day mind
though but.' Another good punctuation is '**or waat?**' as in 'Ye
gannin' on the hoy, or waat?'

A good rule of thumb is never to pronounce the **ing** at the end
of a word. Just make it **in'** or even just '**n** so **getting** becomes

gett'n. And make the **er** at the end of a word into **a** and you won't go far wrong. So **Father** becomes **fatha**. Don't attempt the pitmatic **'fethor'** until you know what you're doing.

The sing-song style of the Geordie accent is very hard to imitate and should be avoided. People who try to do it end up sounding more like the Scandinavians who we got it from.

PUT YER TEETH IN MAN MUTHA MAN...

YE KNAA PICKLES DIVVENT MELT

Schooling methods discourage dialect so children rely on older relatives and their peers to keep it alive. Recent television programmes including Byker Grove, although set in Newcastle, employed quite a few young Wearsiders - presumably because the rest of the country wouldn't notice. The effect this has had on our youngsters is to blend even more elements into our depleted language. Mind, the same youngsters call chips 'fries' and sarnies 'subs' so what chance have we got of hanging on to our beloved dialect? Having said that, my generation was brought up with Cheyenne, Bonanza and Highway Patrol and it had no effect whatsoever on us. We knew it was not our language and we could imitate it but rarely used it in speech, other than when we were playing **coyboys!**

New housing and the spread of small villages has resulted in an amalgamation of areas throughout the north and accounts for inter-breeding of the various dialects. Some people say **'cowld'** and some say **'caad'** some say **'towld'** and some say **'telt'** -all of which are acceptable and in everyday use. **'Owld' 'aad'** and even **'oald'** (with very nearly two syllables) are all interchangeable in our modern integrated community. In fact caad is used for cold except when it refers to the illness – 'Divvent get caad, ye'll catch a cowld.'

Another characteristic sound we are losing is the **'or'** pronunciation of the word ending **'er'** for example **'blether'** (to gossip) would once be pronounced **'blethor'** but is now more commonly **'blethah'** (except perhaps in deepest, darkest Northumberland and Durham – affectionately referred to as woolyback country.) Similarly **'clittor-clattor'** is more likely to be pronounced **'clitta-clatta'**

There are combinations of words which only Geordies use. **Might** and **could** are used together - 'You **might could** mek it if you run.' And the use of the word **can** (pronounced cun) in sentences which should really have 'be able to' so 'I won't be able to visit' becomes 'Aa'll not cun visit' Again this isn't bad grammar, the Old English for **'able to'** is **'cunnan.'** Actually, this manner of speech is used in some of the southern states of America. Obviously the ones pioneered by Geordies!

AA THOWT AA HORD INJUNS
BUT THEN IT WENT AALL QUIET

There are three ways to pronounce **no** in Geordie. There's the very abrupt **na**, the more kindly **nar** and the very definite emphatic **no** which definitely means No! The latter is pronounced with a diphthong and sounds more of a **no-uh**.

Apart from a few exceptions, the Geordie language is the correct way to speak in this part of the country, using words, phrases and grammar handed down to us. There will always be those who say **'He has went'** because they've heard uneducated people saying it. **'He could of'** instead of **'he could have'** and there is a tendency to say **tret** instead of **treated**. That's just lazy and puts us in the same category as Cockneys who use 'firty-free' instead of thirty-three.

One last oddity which may interest you is the use of **r** instead of **t** in the middle of some sentences:

<blockquote>
You berra norra had – I hope you didn't
Worrit's aboot like – Let me explain
Worraboorabirraburra on yer breed – Butter anyone?
</blockquote>

I'm told this quirk probably started in the shipyards, quickly spreading along both sides of the Tyne to the Toon and only recently reaching into the woollyback and pitmatic areas. Glasgow comedians like Stanley Baxter use a very similar pronunciation but it follows slightly different rules.

A Quick Guide

- Words ending **ing** should be pronounced without the **g**.
- **Can't**, **won't** and **don't** should be replaced with **cannet, winnet** and **divvent**. The final **t** is silent if followed by a consonant.
- The word **my** is pronounced **me**. Except when you're angry and have to say 'That is **my** pint!'
- The **a** in words like **have, take** and **make** is pronounced more comfortably **e**, making - **hev, tek** and **mek**.
- In Extreme Geordie, words like **very** and **determined** are more easily pronounced **varry** and **detarrmined**.
- Remember that **keel** is not **key** with an **l** on the end!
- Pronounce **hoo** and **noo** with a U as in **hut** so it's **huw** and **nuw** - Or you'll sound Scottish 'Och aye the noo'

- The word **You** is prononced **yee, ee** or **yu** depending on the context - 'It was yee, yu begger!'
- All sentences should be, and usually are, terminated with the words **like**, **mind**, **tho**, **man** or **but** - or any combination of these. Important sentences should be started with the word **Eeh** or even better **Eeeeh**.
- Words ending in the **o** sound should never be pronounced with even the slightest hint of the English **w** on the end. So **throw** is **thro**. **Crow** is **cro**.
- Remember the wide Geordie grin when pronouncing **e** and **a** as in beer - **Beeah!**

- Words ending in **er** are pronounced with an **a**. So **dinner** becomes **dinna, December** is **Decemba**.
- Words like **find** and **blind** rhyme with **skinned**.
- Say **O** as in **pot**. Then say **hot** without the **t**. This should give you **o-ho**. It means yes. There's no other way of writing it!
- There is no such thing as Newky Brown.
- The word S*nd*rl*nd should not be used except in emergencies.
- Try to make a sentence sound like it's all one word. If people don't understand, say it quicker.
- The rude four letter word beginning with F is delivered with twice the venom and clout in Geordie, so is only needed half as much. This is probably good for the planet.

Geordie Casbalanca

Here's an excerpt from the original Geordie screenplay of Casablanca. If you have it on DVD you can play this bit and read along with it....

RICK HAS BEEN DRINKING HEAVILY. HE SITS AT A TABLE IN THE EMPTY BAR. SAM IS TINKLING THE PIANO NEARBY

RICK BANGS HIS FIST DOWN ON THE TABLE

Rick
Of aall the boozahs in aall the toons in aall the world,
she gans an' waalks into mine...

Whaat the hell's that yer playin'?

Sam
Buggered if aa knaa!

Rick
Wey givower. Ye knaa what aa want t' hear.

Sam
Nar aa divvent.

Rick
Ye played it for hor! Ye can play it for me!

Sam

Er, aa'm not ower sure. Aa might've forgettn it.

Rick

If she can stand it aa can! Play it!

Sam

Owt ye say, Gaffer.

SFX

SLOW ROMANTIC VERSION OF CUSHY BUTTERFIELD
ON PIANO

CUT TO: RICK AND ILSA IN CAR....

SFX

FULLER AND MORE UP-TEMPO MUSIC

CUT TO: BROWN ALE BOTTLE OPENS

Rick

Anyhuw, What's the crack? Tell iz aall aboot yersel.
Whaddya dee? Whaddya think?

Ilsa

Give ower. Aa thowt aa telt ye. Nee questions.

THEY CHINK THEIR GLASSES TOGETHER

Rick

Here's luckin' at ye pet!

Toon and Wear Rivalry

It's a mistake to think that the rivalry between Newcastle and S*nd*rl*nd is purely based on the fact that we have a superior football team. Okay, at the time of writing, the Mackems have won the FA cup most recently, but if we were to give two points for winning the cup and one point for being runners up, Newcastle are currently leading 17 - 6.

No, the rivalry goes back a lot further. Newcastle and S*nd*rl*nd were on opposing sides during the English Civil War AND the Jacobite wars. It was during the Hanoverian/Jacobean conflict that Geordies and Jamies were the names given to opposing sides. Actually for a while they were Jammies which is a bit closer to the mark, especially when referring to Ruud Gullit's last match as Newcastle's manager. As mentioned elswhere in this book, the majority of North Easteners are proud to be called Geordies - except those who support S*nd*rl*nd. And whereas we would love to include Steve Cram in our list of famous Geordies for services rendered to sport in our area, Steve has made it clear on several occasions that he supports the team from the dark place. What's that all about Steve?

One theory about how S*nd*rl*nd got its name, harks back to the days when Newcastle was leading the world in industry and innovation. It was decided that only clever people were allowed to live on Tyneside. Anyone not meeting the required standard of intelligence was cast 'asunder' and a special town had to be built to accomodate them. A settlement known as Asunder-land developed on the banks of the Wear where inferior ships and sub-standard beer could be produced. The name was eventually shortened to S*nd*rl*nd and for those who inhabit the place, and can't cope with long words, shortened further to Sunlund. That's a whole page devoted to a town only rarely and reluctantly mentioned by Geordies.

The Hitchy Dabbas Rocket

A modern Hitchy Dabbas layout. As drawn by Matthew Woods from St Cuthberts School, Walbottle.

What is Hitchy Dabbas?

Hitchy Dabba's is the Geordie name for Hopscotch. It's an energetic children's game originally developed as a training exercise by the Roman soldiers in this area. A grid of squares is 'scotched' on the ground using chalk or charcoal and numbered 1-12. It's easier to play the game on flagstones, which are already laid in an ideal pattern - then you just need numbers.

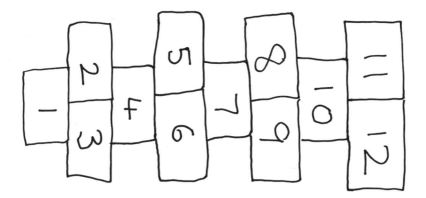

The Dabba is a palm-size piece of flat stone or slate which is thrown to each square in turn. It has to land within the lines. Then, hopping and skipping from one foot to two, avoiding the square in which the dabba has landed, the player moves up the grid, turns at the top and picks up the dabba on the return journey. The winner is the first person to land their dabba in the twelfth square and return.

Obviously the higher numbers are further away and harder to land your dabba within the lines.

Classic Geordie Humour

The problem with Geordie jokes, I've found, is that you can't write them down very well. They have to be passed on by word of mouth because it is the sound of our unique dialect that often makes them so funny.

There are the classic jokes of which we are all so proud; I think Bobby Thompson made a version of this one famous.....

Geordie had a bad leg and called the doctor out. The doctor says, in perfect English, 'Can you walk?' 'Work?' says Geordie, 'I cannot even waalk'

See the problem? That means nothing to people who don't realise that the English '**Walk**' rhymes with the Geordie '**Work**' and the Geordie '**Waalk**' ...well, doesn't really rhyme with any English word - just other Geordie ones like **taalk**, **squaawk** and **chaalk**. And just to dispel a few myths, Bobby Thompson had a Mackem accent not a Geordie one. He was born at Penshaw.

There's the famous joke I first heard told by Tyneside's top comedian, Little Billy Fane, about the motorist who phoned the garage to say there's smoke coming from under his bonnet. The mechanic says 'Is it ower-heatin'?' to which he replies 'No, it's on Gosforth High Street.'

That's a joke that wouldn't travel much further south than Low Fell - although there's a Heaton in Bolton so you could try it next time you're down there.

Billy Fane can also be credited with the reverse-dialect joke of the Geordie who broke down in London. He was under the bonnet of his car when a little lad ran out of a nearby paper shop. Geordie says 'Go and ask if he's got any pliers.' The boy disappeared into the shop and returns saying (in Cockney) 'No, he's got Benson and Hedges though.'

To research classic Geordie humour you need to look first at the works of Geordie Ridley, Tommy Armstrong, Ned Corvan and

AA THOWT YE SAID FETCH A BORD!!

Joe Wilson who were all big-name writers and performers in the mid-19th century music halls. All but Armstrong died tragically young but left us hundreds of entertaining songs, poems, recitations and monologues. They also provided a fascinating insight into the social comment and protest of that era. You can find a couple of their works later in the book.

The advent of radio brought us humour from the rest of the

country and even though the likes of Al Read made the northern accent acceptable to southerners, it was a North West accent. Stanley Holloway, a cockney, started reciting monologues in a northern accent too - again a mix of Yorkshire and Lancashire. Apart from Jimmy James' stooge, Eli Woods, there were no north-east or Geordie voices heard.

This was rectified in the fifties when 'Wotcheor Geordie' arrived on the BBC. Local comedians and actors including Bobby Thompson, Dick Irwin, Chislett (Joe) Ging and Gilbert Scott had their hilarious routines complemented with Tyneside songs and music. Jack Robson composed the theme song 'Where-ivver Ye Gan Yor Sure To Find A Geordie' for this programme. The words taken from his original, signed manuscript can be found later in this book.

Then came the immortal - and quite often mortal Scott Dobson who brought us the 'Larn Yersel Geordie' series of books, dictionaries, records, mugs and tea towels.

George House and Mike Neville, a couple of well-spoken television presenters with the ability to 'lay it on thick' performed a fair bit of Scott's work and opened our ears to Geordie humour at it's best. For instance:

The policeman arrived and said he was following up a report of shooting in the woods 'Shootin'?' says Geordie 'Aa nivvor oppened me mooth!'

Heather Ging produced a regional television show entitled 'What Fettle' which again showcased local humour and music. It's very rare for such programmes to get a national audience though.

It was the workingmen's clubs that admirably carried the burden of keeping our humour alive when TV and radio schedulers lost interest.

Again, Bobby Thompson, one of the most famous comedians, was joined on the circuit by Bobby Pattinson, The Dixielanders,

Lambert and Ross, Spike Rawlings, Bobby Knoxall, Billy Fane, Brian Lewis and many more.

It was Alan Snell who reckoned that the difference between Wonderloaf and an Alsatian is that they're two different breeds. More jokes along the same lines are:

Two Geordie donkeys in a rowing boat. One says 'Ee-aw' and the other one says 'Nar! Ye oar!'

'Doctor, me left oxter smells of coconut' 'Wey it's Bountee'

'Did ye knaa Mork was a Geordie? No? Wey ye knaa nuw!'

'D'ye knaa any card games?' 'Aye, Ice hockey'

It was Brendan Healey who informed us that the Sea-Life Centre would be closed Tuesday mornings for training porpoises.

Like classic songs of yesteryear, these jokes will never go out of fashion. Geordies will never get sick of them. This was allegedly illustrated by the ill-fated comedian who had to stand in for a gig for which Bobby Thompson hadn't turned up. The unfortunate lad was paid off at half time. The audience hadn't laughed at one gag. The concert chairman consoled the poor performer 'Divvint worry son. It's just cos the've nivvor hord yer jokes afore.'

The demise of the clubs threatened the momentum. Folk clubs had been doing their bit since the 60s. Johnny Handle, Malcolm Collins and Mike Elliott were the big names entertaining audiences with not just the humour but also the pathos of the sadly declining pit villages.

Television took another interest in our area when writers Dick Francis and Ian Le Frenais brought us 'The Likely Lads.' The country fell in love with the Geordie voice again, despite the lack of an authentic Newcastle accent from any of the cast. 'Auf Wedersehen, Pet' by the same writing team, brought us three proper Geordies with Jimmy Nail, Tim Healy and Kevin Whateley and this provided the roots from which several Tyneside dramas and comedies have grown. The authentic dialect thrives today with high-profile presenters Ant & Dec, Jayne Middlemiss and Donna Air. It's noticable that most reality shows have a token Geordie and they always do really well.

In the 80s and 90s, the very successful Newcastle comedy clubs stepped in to resurrect our humour nationally. The Toon is now a major venue on the comedy circuit and has spawned a new batch of comedians including Ross Noble, Dave Johns, Mike Milligan, Gavin Webster, Sarah Millican, Barrie Hall, John Fothergill and many more.

Geordie humour is derived from various origins. There is the mickey-taking sarcasm of the working-man developed in the shipyards and pits, motor trade and building trade. This revolves around the simple life and demands of the average club-ganner, the poverty, the comradeship and of course the years of social isolation our unique area and dialect has enjoyed. The cloth cap, whippets and poverty have been replaced by the much referred to 'new underclass' of charvas (pronounced chav in the rest of the country.) Brought up on a diet of confrontational reality TV and yobbish role models, these rip-off sportswear-clad youngsters, fuelled by cheap lager and tabs, provide us with a new target of ridicule. And in the same way as the Belgians joke about the Dutch, the Welsh about the English, we have our own stock of Mackem jokes. I could have copied out a thousand Irish jokes and converted them but that would've been too easy. In our increasingly politically correct world it may have been teetering on the edge of racism.

Another good focus for local humour is exaggerating the pitmatic speech of people from Ashington, Bedlington etc. In fact, the characteristic dialect starts just north of Longbenton around the pit villages of Killingworth, Burradon, Delaval, Seghill etc. The older generations here pronounce both **O** and **U** as **Ur.** So **dog** becomes **durg, Home** becomes **hurm** and **pub** becomes **purb.** The character Ruth, in 'The Archers' is often parodied to exclaim 'Oh no!' in an almost pitmatic style though to our ears she has an accent more typical of the west end. It's also typical of Biffa Bacon in the Viz comic who has been known to build a **snurman** out of **snur.**

This quirk of vowel pronunciation spawned the famous joke of the woman asking for a perm and the hairdresser reciting 'I wandered lonely as a cloud....' And more recently George Welch's unfortunate pal who failed his driving test for hitting a kerb. 'I didn't even knaa it was Burb-a-Jurb week' he said. Similarly, my friend Mick Stobbs is frequently referred to as 'Mixed Herbs.' This makes the Ashington dialect one of the most incomprehensible to outsiders. Here are some examples:

Curd (English) a milk by-product
Curd (Ashington) a fish often eaten with chips
Cord (English) a fine piece of string
Cord (Ashington) a milk by-product

Perk (English) an additional benefit
Perk (Ashington) done to an eye with a finger
Pork (English) the flesh of a pig
Pork (Ashington) an additional benefit

Herd (English) collective noun for cattle
Herd (Ashington) used for carrying bricks
Horde (English) a crowd
Hord (Ashington) collective noun for cattle

Curl (English) to twist or roll the hair
Curl (Ashington) a fossil fuel
Call (English) to speak loudly
Corl (Ashington) to twist or roll the hair

Bird (English) a feathered creature
Burd (Ashington) a partially opened leaf or flower
Board (English) a flat piece of timber
Bord (Ashington) a feathered ceature

Burn (English) to set fire to
Burn (Ashington) a bread roll
Born (English) from birth
Born (Ashington) to set fire to

Other confusing Ashington words:

Slurp – an incline
Flame – mucus coughed up from the throat
Pain – a writing implement
Jerk – a funny tale
Term – a boy's name. Short for Thomas

It's interesting that Peter Sellers decided to portray Clouseau with a French accent including quite a few Ashington words. Don't believe me? Listen to the way he pronounces 'phone' 'home' and 'you know.'

Having learned a little about the history of our area, our language and our strange pronunciations, the next section of the book will jog a few memories with some examples of our weird and wonderful Geordie sayings.

Geordie Sayings

Thank you to family and friends for helping me remember a lot of these. They're things my Nanna Hogg and Auntie Zela would say and things I overheard in the Red Stamp Stores at Benwell where I delivered 'Rations' as a schoolboy. Twenty years in the motor trade where the humour is as rife as any industry and a parallel thirty years on the music scene, rubbing shoulders with the funniest people in the country around the pubs and clubs of the North East, provided many more gems. I'm sure there are more. These are just the ones I've heard.

Chaalkin' on the bleezer
Not speaking to each other

Gettin' off at Manors
Not finishing the job – Method of birth control

Wey aa'll stand tappin'
I'm flabbergasted. That is a surprise!

He couldn't hit a coo's arse with a banjo!
He's not a very good darts player

Givower plodgin!
You have stepped over the line (In darts)

Byker Teacake
Head butt

Huw's it hingin'?
How's life treating you?

Aadivvenwannee
I'd rather not

Yedivvenhattee
You don't have to

Eegannin?
Are you going?

Eeganaganwiwu?
Would you like to come with us?

You waddn't pinch a tettie off her plate
She's quite scary

Caad as a well-digger's welly
Quite cold

Aa haven't got a pot to pee in
nor a windah to hoy it oot!
I have very few possessions

He's a reet heed-the-baall
He's mad as a hatter

S'narf snaa'n
It is snowing heavily

Wuz want fer nowt 'cept what wuz haven't got and
what wuz haven't got wuz divvint even want
We're fine thankyou

Ye cannot ride two bikes wi' one arse
You are taking on too much work

Lace curtains an' kippers
All for show

Givin' it six nowt
Putting in maximum effort

He's as thick as ten netty lids
He's not very bright

You'd mek a better door than a windah
You're standing in front of the television

Gan canny else ye'll get chinned
Be careful, you may get beaten up

The chippy's stowed off th' neet
The chip shop is busy tonight

He couldn't shoot coal
He's not a very good singer

He couldn't draa breath
He's not a very good artist

He's as much use as two blokes short
He isn't much help

He's as much use as a back pocket in a vest
He isn't much help

Aa'm full as a boot, me
I've had sufficient to eat

Wuz'll lowp ower yon dyke an' nick some snadgies
We'll climb over the wall and steal some turnips

Me da's gannin' 'is ends
My father is shouting angrily

Will ye tek a few broth?
Would you like a bowl of soup?

Face like a yard o' tripe
Doesn't look amused

There's not many like'im diff'rent
He's one in a million

Tappy Lappy
Quickly

Face like a borst pomegranate
Quite spotty

That's yer place on the bus
That is your destiny in life

Any amoont
Quite a few

Ye divven' knaa nowt ye
You haven't a clue

The aad gadgy couldn't stop a pig in a passage
He has bandy legs

Not ower clivvor
Feeling poorly or not right

Geordie alarm clock
Early morning flatulence from a partner

Aa'm sweatin' like a swamp donkey
It's rather hot in here

Huw!
Excuse me!

Nuw!
Good morning. Are you well?

He's gorra berra job than the pollis in the park
He has quite an easy job

Aa divvent knaa if aa'm in the park or at the pictures
I'm confused

Aa'm fair clammin'
I'm very thirsty

Yer meggin' but?
You can't be serious

Yer gannin' six an ites but?
No really, you can't be serious. Usually followed with…

Hadaway an' cack
I don't believe you

Caad enuff for yer flannins
You may need your thermal underwear

He's intrestin' as a pund o' suet
He's quite dull

Like a one-armed paperhanger wi' an itchy arse!
Quite busy

Abackabeyont
A long way out of town

He's cowped his creels
He has fallen over

It winnet gan backower
My reverse gear isn't working

Five-finger discoont
Shoplifting

Gateshead hankie
Blowing one's nose in the street without a handkerchief

Doonbye
Not too far away

Ootbye
Further out of town

What fettle?
How are you?

Showin' yer browtens up
Displaying bad manners

Givower howkin' yer sneck
Don't pick your nose

Ye clocked the kite on him?
Have you noticed his large waistline?

Luckih!
Now pay attention!

These bullets are ower claggy
These sweets are too sticky

Aa'm just on me jack
I'm alone

Cuddyload
A large amount

Nigh enuff for pitwork
Accurate enough

The bairn's bowked 'is boilie
The child has vomited

Yon chep's howked 'is bangle
That gentleman has vomited

Chuffed as a fuzzy button
Very pleased with the result

Wor lass's gorra monk on
My wife isn't speaking to me

The bonna's ahaad
The bonfire has been lit

Me kek's is aall clarty
My trousers are muddy

He's gorra handshake like a deed cuddy's tongue
He's something of a wimp

Black as inside a bull's gut wi' its tail doon
It's very dark

He thinks he's it an' a bit, him
He has delusions of grandeur

Gannin' oot on the hoy
Going out for a drink

Gannin' oot on the lash
Going out for a drink

Gannin' oot tommin'
Going for a drink in the hope of encountering the opposite sex

Clockin' the blart
Checking out the female talent

Clockin' the totty
Checking out the opposite sex

She's gorra hintend like a Cullercoats donkey
She's overweight

It's good watter ruined
This tea is rather weak

Whaat's the crack?
What's going on?

Aa've gettn me darza new ganzie hacky
My lovely new sweater is dirty

The dickynorse gi' wor young'un a note
My younger brother has headlice

Bleachindoon
A blizzard of snow, sleet or rain

Ye been gettn a club oot?
Did you buy that on hire purchase?

It's puttin' in dowley
It's getting dark

Where ye beetlin' off tee nuw?
Is this you going out again?

Wor lass's fell wrang
My wife is pregnant

He's like a hoose end
He's very large

Skinchies
Call a truce

Geet canny like owt
Pleasant

Tart's bathwatter
Earl Grey Tea

Penny Floater
Cheap plastic football

Aa could chow the arse off a low-flyin' duck
I'm very hungry

Stottindoon
Heavy rain

Waalkin' like a dog on wet lino
Unsteady

Me oxters is fair hotchin'
I need underarm deodorant

His leeks's barely scallions
He has a poor crop of leeks

The Hoosey's full o' gannies
The bingo is popular with the older ladies

Aa'm sick on't
I'm fed up with the whole affair

Wor lass'll tek the gully tiv iz!
My wife will chase me with the carving knife

He's aanly had the howdie's wesh
The last time he was washed was by the midwife

Me gannie was passed horsel
My grandmother was worried sick

There's a rabbit off mind
Something isn't quite right

Divvent fash yersel
Don't trouble yourself

Ye've got more patter than the rain
You talk rubbish

Workie ticket
An irritating person

Yer scran's kizzened
Your dinner is burnt

Haad yer blaah
Hold on a moment

Aa'm aallower scumfished me
I'm hot and sweating

Haad yer whisht
Be quiet

He's a reet blethorskite
He talks rubbish

Aavinaa
I do not know

Gerrim telt
Chastise him

Keep a'haad
Take care

Modern Geordie Terms

Belta - Very good

Charva Cava - Cheap sparkling wine

Kappa slappa - Charva girl

Geet lush - Very good

Geet manka - (Noun) Big, horrible thing

Geet manky - (Adj) Horrible

Geet narly - Very large

Geet canny like owt - Pleasant

Geet radgie - Very annoyed

Geet mingin' - Very smelly

Bizzies - Police

Cushty bardy - Good

Divvent alfie on wu - Don't tell anyone what we did

Lush, Mint, Sweet, Random - Good

Couple eff - Let me have a smoke of your tab

Fog blah - Let me have first smoke of your tab

Doiler, Doilum - Idiot

Hoisty - Stolen

Kets - Sweets

Cooncil Telly - Terrestrial Television

Tickheed - Person wearing a Nike baseball cap

TICKHEED

Extreme Geordie

So far we have concentrated on Geordie as it is spoken today. However, listening closely to the more elderly residents of Northumberland we can get an idea of how our ancestors may have sounded. Listen out for the word **taken** pronounced **tyun** or **chun** and **chep** for **man** and **syun** for **soon**. The word **Hinny** for instance is an ideal term of endearment for either sex. It rolls off the tongue of pensioners in Bedlington but seems awkward for younger people to use or even hear. It's a precious word that should really be protected.

The pitmatic speech already mentioned contributed more to our vocabulary than pronunciation. The words used such as **crackett**, **kist**, **hunkers** etc., were adopted by miners in town, up the river and down into Durham but the pronunciation differed.

Extreme Geordie, which is the hardest for non-natives to understand, utilises vowel sounds we've already associated with Ashington and adds a spectacular pronunciation of R.

The guttural, Northumbrian R or burr as it's known, possibly evolved from Flemish, French or German influences. There are certainly hints of it in their modern speech. Some say it was fashionable to copy the speech impediment of an early Duke of Northumberland but if that's the case, it's more likely people were copying the speech of one of our Hanoverian kings.

It's a gargling, percussive, uvular sound coming from somewhere between the throat, tongue and the roof of the mouth. Some say it starts with an H some say CH or even G. The nearest I can get to explain the sound is to listen to a Scotsman pronounce **loch**. The CH is pronounced not as CK but in the same way a Liverpudlian pronounces the CK in chicken. It's almost a cockling attempt to bring up phlegm. The Geordie word **hockle** is a good onomatopoeia as it sounds like the action it describes.

Try snoring through your mouth as you breathe in; now try

the same breathing outwards. Now replace all the Rs in the following sentence with that sound... 'Arund the rugged rocks the ragged rascal raan.'

It's also used in the middle of words; 'worry' or 'horrible' are good examples. There's also a hint of it in the final R of words like the Northumbrian 'fethor' meaning father.

Several years ago I interviewed evacuees from World War ll as part of a reminiscence therapy project. I visited several care homes and sheltered accommodation listening to the wartime memories. One Burradon lady in her seventies recalled:

'There'd been an air raid the neet afore and theor was a geet crater in the road. Wey they nivvor sorted it an' this lorry hirrit in the blackoot and the sides borst oppen. It was carryin' oranges and they aall spilt oot and went rollin doon the road'

She continued telling the story of families rushing from their homes to gather the oranges; a rarity in those days. The word 'orange' in Northumbrian is almost unidentifiable. That and the word lorryload were being used two or three times in a sentence as the story gathered pace. The sound recordist that day was Claire Pollard, a well-spoken southerner. As she twiddled the knobs I could see she didn't have the slightest clue what she was recording. Listening to the tape later I understood why.

The Northumbrian R is in danger of extinction. There was a time when children learning from their elders, often misheard and developed a speech impediment pronouncing R as W. They'd never heard it enunciated correctly!

An excellent example of Extreme Geordie can be heard by listening to a fine singer, Brian Watson. He has recordings but seeing him live is a real treat, as you get to hear him introducing his songs in that manner too. I defy anyone south of Doncaster to decipher the lyrics when Brian is in full swing. You'll need extreme Geordie to sing the old songs that appear later in the book.

Ten Commandments

(As handed down to Moses Thompson at
Mount Pleasant Club - yonks ago)

1 Thou shalt have no other team but the Toon.

2 Thou shalt not make grave mistakes.
(Like getting' lost in S*nd*rl*nd wearin' a
Toon top.)

3 Thou shalt not take Alan Shearer's name in vain.

4 Remember which is match day and keep it free.

5 Honour your fatha and mutha that they'll still
be around till you find someone else to look
after you.

6 Thou shalt not fettle nee one proper like
- even workie tickets.

7 Thou shalt not play away wi' spare totty.

8 Thou shalt not nick nowt.

9 Thou shalt not bare false teeth.

10 Thou shalt not covet thy neighbour's season
ticket or his whippet or his wife's ass.

A Job Well Done
From 'Fairly Truthful Tales'

Me sivvinth borthday we'd a party at wor hoose
Wi fowerteen kids from wor class
We had charades and cheese scones and jelly
And a bloke come to cut off the gas

Now me da, like ye knaa, was cornbeef in one lug
'Cut the grass' is what he thowt he'd said
It was 'Bob-a-Job' week and Da bein' generous like
Sez 'Aalreet, bonny lad, gan ahead'

He'd a long mac, smelt of stagnant owld floorcloths
He didn't look nowt like a scout
And he had nee short pants and nee beret
Nee badges, nee woggle, nee nowt!

He went into the cupboard under wor stairs
Me da was puzzled but says 'Mind yer head,
If yer lookin' for the mower we've not got one,
You'll have to use clippers instead'

The bloke seemed to manage wi' the tools that he had
A pair of pliers and a geet rusty spanner
And me da reached deep in 'is pocket
And give him a couple o' tanners

It was when ma went to mek me da's dinner
That she noticed the gas wasn't on
Cos the chips were still white after nigh-on an hoor
So he had to have jelly and scones

And when he complained, me mutha went mad
Aa thowt she was gannin' to kill
She smacked me da roond the heed wi' the chip pan
Cos it was his job to pay aall the bills

The next morn' aa got up for waggin' off school
But aa couldn't get oot the back door
Cos me da had 'is heed in the oven
And 'is legs stretched aall ower floor

Aa had to climb ower and squeeze mesel' oot
Cos he hadn't left ower much space
But aa got him a cushion to put under 'is heed
Cos he was gettin' a ridge on 'is face

Aa'd to help oot me ma mekkin' dinner that neet
She was spoilin', I think, for a fight
She was still in a huff onaccoonter the gas
And me da, 'course, just kept oot o' sight

She was heatin' up peas in the kettle
While aa had to stand up a height
Aa was broonin' the top of a big shepherds pie
By howldin' it under the light

After tea me ma sat on the piana stool
In the corner where the piana once stood
Hummin' Rachmaninov's piana concerto
As close to C minor as she could

It was then that wuz noticed the piana had gone
Cos it should've been stood standin' there
Da sez 'Aa've selt it and paid that daft gas bill'
She says 'Eeh! Aa'll gan to the foot o' wor stairs!'

He says 'Divvent get yer liberty bodice in a twist,
It's at the paanshop on Bolinbroke Street,
Aa'll be strite back up there on payday'
An' he proved it by showin' the receipt

She got up from the stool in a temper
Like she was gannin' to thump him some more
Cos she picked up her banjo by the thin end
But he was saved by a knock at the door

It was the bloke in the mac an' the pliers stood there
And me da thowt 'Mind, this Boy Scout's willin'
He says 'See if you can sort oot me gas, son,
An aa'll see if aa can find yer a shillin'

So that evenin' was aall peace and quiet
Wi' me ma and me da just sat there
Listenin' to Billy Cotton on the wireless
Then suddenly, da jumps oot 'is chair

He says 'That bloody Boy Scout's an impostor!
Aa've just been sat here workin' out,
That bugger's done me for two shillins,
And wuz nivvor got a sticker nor nowt!'

Geordie Jokes

I remember one day Prince Charles was visiting our village. They'd been out and cut the grass verge, painted the lamppost, fixed the glass in the telephone box and washed the rude word off the bus shelter. The Prince went on a bit walkabout and he comes up to Jonty. He says 'I must say, this is a very smart village.' Jonty says 'Aye, it's aalreet th'day but ye'll have to come back one day when you're not heor!'

He went to the next bloke. I don't know who it was. He says 'It's a beautiful day, isn't it?' and the bloke just says 'Aa divvint knaa. Aa divvint live heor.'

There's two pubs in the village: The Riveters Arms and the Plodgeborough Arms. Nobody goes to the Plodgeborough Arms cos it's always stowed off.

It's just a little village. The population's been nigh on the same for fifty years. That's likely because every time a baby's born some bloke has to leave town.

Jonty was polishing his bike lamp when a genie appeared. 'You are my master' he shouts. Jonty says 'Div aa get three wishes, like?' The genie says 'Nar, we're cuttin' back. Ownly one nuwadays.' So Jonty says 'Wey, whaat'll aa wish for?' The genie says 'What if aa cure aall yer ills? Like, mek yer bad back better and yer gammy leg and yer arthuritis?' 'Naargh!' sez Jonty, 'Nick off! Aa'm on Incapacity Benefit, man!'

Dodgy Ray went to the fancy dress ball at the middle club last Christmas. He wore horns on his head, a big rubber udder hanging between his legs, his number eleven Toon top and he carried his young'un's toy machine gun. 'What ye come as, Dodger?' says the concert chairman. 'Is it not obvious?' says Dodger, 'I'm a right-wing military coo.'

Wor young'un was at school the other day and Miss Simpkins, the one with the nose hair, says 'Who can give me a sentence with the word *sleep* in it?' So wor young'un says 'Last neet me had a nightmare so me sleep wi' Mammy and Daddy.' So Miss Simpkins tutted and she says 'No, ….Last night *I* had a nightmare so *I slept* with Mammy and Daddy.' So wor young'un was confused like. He says 'Wey that musta been after me went to sleep but.'

There was one owld pit pony at Ashington that used to kick out every time its lugs caught the top of the stable door. Geordie was so sick; he started chiselling away at the frame. Billy says 'Wad it not be easier just shovelin' the floor away?' He says 'Divvent be soft. It's 'is lugs that's ower lang. Not 'is legs.'

Two young lads carried their mate into Wansbeck General. 'Oh aye!' says the nurse 'What's ee done this time? Glue sniffin? Smack? Coke?' One of the lads looked a bit sheepish and said 'No, we're skint, man. He's been through me ma's spice rack.' He took half a dozen bottles out of his pocket and put them on the desk. There was Ground Coriander, Garam Masala, Cumin, Fenugreek, Turmeric and Cardamoms. 'D'you think ee'll be aalreet, Norse?' 'Aye, Pet,' she says. 'Ee's ganna be in a kurma for a coupla days but.'

**AA'VE FINISHED YER NEW COAT RACK, PET.
AA'M AWAY TO THE PUB**

Dodgy Ray and his missus were checking their lottery tickets. They had one each. 'Dodger?' says his missus, 'Would yer still love iz if you won ten million pund?' 'Wey course aa wad, Pet,' he reassured her, 'Aa'd miss ye, mind.'

Mind he's always been a ladies man, Dodger. That's cos he can't be bothered going out the back to the Gents.

There was once Jonty went to the doctors and told him about his bad foot, his dodgy knee, his sore tummy, his bad back and the headaches he keeps getting. Then he told him about his cough and his bad chest, the ringing in his ears and his sore throat. The doctor listened to all his complaints and says 'Your main problem is hypochondria.' Jonty says 'Ah, nar! Aa hevvn't gettn that an'aall hev aa?'

After Jonty's daughter was born he was straight on the phone to me. 'It's a lassie!' he shouts, 'Sivin pund twelve. Looks just like her da!' I says 'That's aalreet, Man. As lang as she's healthy.'

Miss Simpkins, the one with the nose hair and the neck-lump was introducing the infant class to bible studies. She says 'Who can tell me which is the biggest, best and most important book in the whole wide world?' Wor young'un puts up his hand and says 'Please, Miss. Is it the Argos catalogue?'

On the great wagon train taking pioneers out to Oregon, my great great great Uncle Tadger was a scout. One evening after a long day's scouting he arrived back at camp. The trail boss said 'Did you see any Indians?' So Tadger says 'Nar. But aa was ootbye up ower yon top side an' aa hord drums.' So the trail boss says 'Were they war drums?' Tadger says 'Nar, aa think they probbly belanged to the injuns.'

YE TELT IZ TO FETCH ME AAN HORSE !

Dodgy Ray took his wife to the Hoppins. The bloke on the dive-bombers says 'If ye can gan on there for ten minutes withoot screamin', ye can hev the ride for nowt.' He was sly mind. He set it off at twice the normal speed. Dodger didn't scream once. When he got off, the bloke congratulated him. Dodger says 'Mind, it was hard. I varnigh screamed when wor lass fell oot!'

Jonty's wife's breath could strip the paint off a netty door. Jonty was usually so mortal that he'd never noticed until their wedding night. But he was embarrassed about his whiffy feet anyway. Apparently, they were getting ready for bed; Jonty took his socks off and hoyed them in the bin. When they got into bed and he was just about to ask how long she'd had her birthmark, she says 'Jonty, aa've got a confession to mek.' He says 'I knaa what you're gan' to say, Pet. You've ett me socks haven't you?'

Because of the increasing fear of bird flu across Europe, the ferry from Newcastle to Amsterdam has had to ban all hen parties.

Mind, Dodgy Ray's a lazy nowt. He even married a lass that was already pregnant. The gaffer was bollockin' him for bein' late the other day. He says 'Ye just live roond the corner. Billy Barras lives fower mile away an' he's aalways on time.' Dodger just says 'Aye, but when Billy gets up late, he's got that far to run he can mek up time.'

Jonty and Dodgy Ray went on a skiing holiday to Austria. They'd never been on skis before. The first day they got to the top and Jonty says 'Wey do we zig forst or zag forst?' 'I nivvor thowt to ask,' says Dodger. Just then they noticed another bloke walking up the hill. So Jonty shouts 'Huw, Marra! D'ye knaa if yer supposed to zig forst or zag forst? The gadgy just looked at them like they were stupid. (So they looked at him back like they weren't.) 'Buggered if aa knaa,' the bloke shoots, in an Austrian accent, 'Aa'm a tobogganist.' Jonty says 'Oh, sorry to bother you. Giz twenty Woodbines while yer on but.'

TO TELL THE TRUTH, PET.
IT DOESN'T EVEN GAN IN ONE EAR

Jonty never liked his sister much. She had three brothers and
he only had two. She was talking to her eldest lad and saying
'Nuw, aa knaa what ye get up to, so just promise yer ma that yer
practisin' safe sex.' He says 'What y'on aboot man mutha man?'
So she says 'Whaat's the forst thing ye should ask a lass afore yuz
mek love?' The poor lad was dead embarrassed. He says 'Er, aa
usually ask what time does yer fatha get in?'

The only reason all these do-gooders complain about people wearing fur coats and don't bother about folks wearing leather is because they're less likely to get chinned by a little old lady than a Hell's Angel.

Anyway, if we were meant to be vegetarian, why do they make animals out of meat?

Jonty went into Bootses to get a bottle for his bad cough. He was back the next day saying it didn't work so they made him up something different. This went on all week. In the end the pharmacist was getting that sick, he made him up a special bottle. Mind, we never heard Jonty coughing for weeks. I thought I should get a bottle, just in case like. When I asked the pharmacist what it was he just laughed. He says 'Aa gave him heavy-duty laxative, man. He daresn't cough!'

The bairn came in from his school football match. I says 'Wey, what was the score?' He says 'Fower-nowt.' So I says 'Whe won but?' He says 'Duh! …The team that scored the fower goals, Stupid!'

Dodgy Ray was taking a shortcut from the Riveters one night. As he stumbled through the park he fell in the pond. He's never been a good swimmer but luckily there was a lad nearby that heard the splash. He jumped in and saved him. Mind, Dodger was so grateful. He says 'Ye just saved me life, Marra. Aa would gi' yer a fiver for a reward but aa've ownly got a tenner on iz.' So the bloke says 'Wey lowp back in and aa'll save ye again.'

Jonty's as much use as a back-pocket in a vest. He took a long dinner break the other day. His boss went looking for him and there he was in the barbers on the High Street. His boss bust in and says 'Huw! Yer not supposed to get yer hair cut in company time!' Quick as a flash Jonty says 'Wey it grew in company time.' So the Gaffer says 'Not aall of it didn't.' So Jonty says 'That's why I'm not gettin' it aall cut off.'

Mind, the last time Jonty scived off work was on account of getting something in his eye. He phoned work and says 'Aa'm blind! A cannot see nowt!' There was nowt wrong with him but he decided to have a few days off anyway. The gaffer was out doing a message and he saw Jonty going into the pictures. He thought 'Reet! Aa've got him this time.' He followed him in to the pictures and followed him to a seat. Jonty was sly though. He saw the gaffer just in time and as they sat down Jonty put his hand on the gaffer's arm and says to him 'S'cuse me, Miss. Does this bus gan t' the General?'

I was talking to Jonty's eldest lad the other night. He says 'Aa've gett'n mesel a new bint. We're courtin' strang.' So I says 'Champion. What's she like?' He says 'Ah, she's porfect, man. Just like me mutha. Aa've aalways wanted to meet a wife just like me mutha.' So I says 'Aa'm dead chuffed for you. What's yer da think of her' He says 'Aa telt you man, she's just like me mutha. He cannot stand the lass.'

When Jonty's young'un went to the big school he came home the first night and says 'Da! Aa've got to decide if aa want to larn French or Jarman.' Jonty says 'Why? Is there a difference like?'

There's people dying nowadays that never died before. When old Alfie Stott was busy dying, he called his wife to his bedside. He says 'Sorry, Pet. Aa've got a confession to mek. Aa once had a fling wi' big Bella from the Riveters.' His wife, Ethel, says 'That's okay, Pet. That's why aa poisoned you.'

He never left her a penny mind. His will read 'I Alfie Stott, being of sound mind, spent the bugger.'

The undertaker asked Ethel what she wanted doing with his ashes. She says 'Oh, just born them an'aall.'

Miss Simpkins, the one with the nose-hair, the neck lump and one short leg was teaching history. She says 'George Washington chopped down his father's cherry tree but his father forgave him. Why do you think that was?' Wor young'un's first with his hand up, 'Please Miss, is it cos he still had an axe in his hand?'

Jonty's lad was snoggin' his lass at the back of the Co-op. She said she'd never had such a passionate, burning hot kiss in her life. He says 'Sorry, Pet. I forgot to tek me tab oot.'

The lass behind the counter at Bootses was on the phone to a customer. She turned to the boss and says 'Aad wifey on the phone wants to knaa if we can deliver incontinence pants?' The boss says 'Aye, nowts th' bother. Ask her where she's ringing from.' The girl asked and told her boss 'She says from the waist doon.'

YE KNAA YER GETTING AAD...

...WHEN YER BORTHDA SUIT NEEDS IRONED

We went to the coast last week and the bairns ran straight for the ice cream van but there was no one serving. They knocked on the windows and shouted. In the end the pollis came and opened the door and climbed inside. There was Toni, the ice cream man, lying stiff as a board. He was covered in monkey-juice, hundreds and thousands, chocolate sprinkles, butterscotch fudge sauce and crushed nuts. He had a flake sticking out each lug. The pollis reckoned he'd topped himself.

Dodger went to the docs. He says 'It's me lugs, Doc. Aa'm gan' cornbeef.' So the doc says 'What's the symptoms?' Dodger says 'It's that cartoon thing on Channel Fower, isn't it?'

Me mate Neil's a cracking photographer. He was invited out for a meal one night to a posh client's house in Jesmond and he took an instant dislike to the wife (Well, it saves time.) She says, posh like, 'Thems were beautiful photographs what you took. You must have a geet good camera.' Just as they were leaving, Neil says 'That was wonderful scran, Pet. You must have some canny pans.'

Two Geordies lost in the desert. One of them says 'Ye knaa what day this is?' 'Buggered if aa knaa.' said his mate. 'It's the Club trip to Plessey Woods, man.' So his mate says 'Wey, they've gettn' a canny day for it.'

The first one says 'I see the Mackems got beat again.' His mate says 'How d'ye knaa?' He says 'Cos its quaarter to five!'

There was one day at Cullercoats, Jonty's bairn got lost. He went to the pollis and says 'I cannot find me fatha.' The pollis says 'What's he like?' So the bairn says 'Beer, tabs, lasses..'

Jonty's car failed its test so he was looking for a new one. His mate was selling an old pick up. 'It's ownly fifteen year owld,' he says, 'Two hunred an' thorty thoosand miles. Nivver been a pick o' bother.' Jonty says 'No thanks. Aa was sorta hopin' for summat that still had its aan teeth.'

ACTUALLY AA'M A BIT OF A LEG MAN AN'AALL

There's a box on the bar in the Riveters that says 'For The Blind.' As soon as it's full they're getting a new blind for the kitchen window.

When me nanna was moving into her council bungalow she put her old piano out in the street with a sign saying 'Free to good home.' There was no one interested. It stood for three days so she put a sign on it that said 'Piano for sale. £100.' It got nicked that same night!

AA WAS HAPPILY MARRIED FOR TWENTY YEAR

WEY, TWENTY OOT O' FOWERTY'S NOT BAD

Miss Simpkins, the one with the nose hair, neck lump, short leg, dodgy cardy and teeth like a broken fence was talking to the class about how animals can't talk like humans. Wor young'un disagreed. He put up his hand, 'Please Miss, wor cat nearly said a rude word once.' Miss Simpkins was fascinated 'Really?' she said. 'Yes Miss. It was in the garden when the Alsatian that lives nextdoor jumped ower the fence. Wor cat said 'Sh…..' but before he finished the word the dog had ett him.'

Dodgy Ray had to go shopping with his wife one day. A stranger came up to them in Eldon Square and said to Dodger's wife 'Can you tell me where the nearest boozah is please?' She nodded towards Dodger and says 'Aye, pet. This is him.'

The circus came to Ashington a few years ago and the man-eating tiger got loose. It started eating one of the clowns but thought he tasted funny so he made a run for it. There was mad panic. People were searching everywhere. Then they found it lying dead just outside Portland Park with Geordie Stott standing over it. The pollis said 'How on earth did you kill it? Did you shoot it?' He says 'Nar, nar. Just jumped on it wi' me club.' The Pollis says 'It must be some size, this club?' Geordie says 'Aye, massive. Nigh on fower hundred members.'

I was in the changing room at the baths and someone's mobile phone started ringing. This bloke presses a button on it and it had a loud speaker. This wife says 'Hello pet, I've just found the most amazing pair of shoes for Sophie's wedding. Only £80 in the sale.' So the bloke says 'Smashin'. I'm dead chuffed for you.' Then she says 'I was passing the travel agents and there was a world cruise on offer for £20,000 should I book it?' So he says 'Wey aye, Pet. Gan for it.' Then she says, 'You know that house we fancied at Darras Hall? Well, it's back on the market and they've dropped the price to £750,000. Should I put an offer in?' He says 'Wey aye, Pet. Gan for it. Champion.' She says 'I love you darling,' then she hung up and the bloke shouts 'Anyone knaa whe's this phone is?'

Miss Simpkins, the one with the nose hair, the neck lump, one short leg and a dodgy cardy was telling the class about evolution. She says 'Man evolved from apes.' Wor young'un, sharp as owt, says 'Please Miss, why've we still got apes then?'

When the vicar, Mr McSomething, was leaving our church for pastures new, old Mrs Wotsername says 'Eeh, taraa Pet. Whoever we get next'll not be as good as ye.' So he says 'Oh, that's kind of you to say so.' She says 'Nar, ivvry vicar we get's worse than the last un!'

The new vicar's wife complained to the council about the bad language used by workmen outside her house. The clerk of the works got the two lads into his office to write out a statement for the board of enquiry. It read 'My colleague was holding a fence post whilst I installed it using a geet mell. One of the blows hit him directly on the head causing multiple fractures. Before he collapsed he remarked 'Silly Billy, do be careful!'

Dodger was going on holiday and Jonty asked him to fetch him some tabs back. When he got back he says, 'There ye gan, bonny lad. Ninety sivin quid you owe iz.' Jonty nearly fell off his chair. 'Whaat? How much? Where'd you gan for yer hols, like?' Dodger says 'Scarborough.'

His lass went to Royal Quays. She fancied a pair of them camouflage trousers - but she couldn't find any.

Three bears had been for a walk along Blyth beach one morning while their porridge was cooling down. When they got back, the baby bear shouts 'Someone's ett me porridge!' Then the mammy bear shouts 'Someone's ett MY porridge!' Then the daddy bear shouts 'Never mind yer stupid porridge! Some bugger's nicked me laptop!'

SHE'S NIVVOR GANNA HEAR A QUID'S WORTH

Dodger's dad was wandering about outside the Riveters the other night. 'What y' up te?' I says. 'Aa'm looking for the bit of chowa aa spit oot last neet,' he says. 'Did you not stick it ahint yer lug like you genly dee?' says I. 'No, aa definitely spit it oot,' he says. 'Ah here, man,' I says, 'Forget it. Have a bit o' beech nut.' He says, 'No thanks marra. I've got to find it. Me top set's still in it!'

Jonty phoned the dentist and asked how much it would cost to get a tooth taken out and was told ninety-five pounds. 'Whaat? Aa cannot afford that, man! Can ye not dee it nee cheaper?' 'Sorry that's the going rate.' said the dentist. So Jonty asks 'What if ye dee it withoot th'anaesthetic, like?' The dentist thought for a while and said, 'That would save you £21.50.' 'Reet,' says Jonty, 'What if ye get one o' yer trainees to dee it instead of ye? That wad work oot a bit cheaper waddn't it?' The dentist had to think, 'Erm, it may be a bit painful but I could knock another thirty pounds off.' 'Champion,' says Jonty, 'That's more like it. But what if ye got the other students in and mek it like a teachin' practise?' 'Well, it might be a bit of a long job and quite traumatic and painful but that is possible - and I would only charge you five pounds.' 'Champion!' says Jonty, 'Can ye book wor lass in for next Thorsday then?'

When posh Auntie Vi came for Sunday dinner she always insisted on someone saying grace before we ate. Last time she was just remarking on how big wor young'un was getting and insisted on him saying grace. He started off by saying 'Thank you God for me mammy and daddy and aall me family.' Auntie Vi was beaming with pride. Then he said 'And thank you God for wor dog and aall me friends at school.' Then he went on 'Thank you for all the lovely food we are about to eat....' then he stopped, hesitated and whispered to his mam 'God'll knaa aa'm fibbin' cos aa hate sprouts!'

The Gas Board bloke knocked on Jonty's front door. Their young'un answered it. He had a tab in his gob, a can of export in one hand, a Playboy in the other and the stereo blasting. The salesman asked 'Is yer mammy or daddy in?' The young'un just said 'Duh?! Does it look like it?'

The police caught a lad walking down the street with Jonty's radiogram under his arm at three o'clock in the morning. Caught him red handed. Jonty called in to the police station the next morning and asked the desk sergeant 'Can aa just have a quick word wi' the lad that borgled wor hoose last neet, please?' The sergeant says 'Sorry, Jonty. That's not allowed. He's locked up like.' 'Aah, gan on, man,' says Jonty. 'No, aa'm sorry,' says the sergeant, 'What d'ye want to see 'im for anyhoo?' 'Oh, aa just want to ask him how he got into wor hoose withoot wakin' wor lass up. Aa've been tryin' to dee it for years.'

Dodger sent his young'un to bed sharp for being naughty. Five minutes later a little voice shouts 'Da-ad. Can aa hev a drink o' watter?' Dodger says 'No ye cannot. You've been ower naughty.' Ten minutes later a little voice says 'Da-ad, please can aa hev a drink o' watter?' Dodger says 'No! Now go to sleep!' Ten minutes later, 'Da-ad, please can aa hev a drink o' watter?' So Dodger says 'If ye say that once more aa'm ganna come in there and bray ye.' Ten minutes later, 'Da-ad, when you come in to bray iz, will you fetch a drink o' watter please?'

Dodger's da was in the doc's getting his ears checked. 'I think I can see the problem,' says the doc, 'You've got a suppository stuck in your ear.' 'Wey, bugger me,' says Dodger's dad, 'That'll explain where me hearin' aid's got te!'

Doris Norris was telling Dodgy Ray's wife 'Course, the beer doesn't agree wi' my husband, ye knaa. And he hasn't got a clue how to play poker.' 'Oh that must be great,' says Dodger's missus. Doris says 'Aye. Wey it wad be, if ownly he waddn't drink and play poker so much.'

Dodgy Ray was in a right fettle the other night. There was a bus trip in from Scotland. 'Them Scottish, ye knaa,' he says, 'Reckon us Geordies are aggressive! Next one that says that's ganna get his heed kicked in!'

Jonty and Dodger went into the Riveters. Jonty says 'Your roond.' Dodger says 'So are ye, yu fat nowt!'

There was this couple sat next to us in the big club last Sunday. All night he was saying things like 'Another Cherry-B, Sweetheart?' and 'Tab, Darlin?' 'Would you like a pickled egg, Loverchops?' 'Could you pass the spare dabba, Flower?' All luvvy-duvvy pet names like. I was next to him out the back and I says 'How long yuz been married then?' He says 'Fowerty years.' I says 'What? An' ye still caall her aall them soppy owld pet names?' He says 'Aye. Tell you the truth, aa've forgettn what she's caalled.'

Two local priests decided to let their hair down one quiet Tuesday. They went on a day out to Plessey Woods. It was deserted as the schools had gone back. It was scorching hot and there was no one around so they thought they might go in skinny-dippin. They splashed about for half an hour but before they could get back to their clothes, all thirty-three members of the Blyth and District Ladies Wild Flower Appreciation Society came past. One of the priests covered his privates but the other one just put his hands over his face. The women screamed and ran. The first priest shouted at the other 'Whaat in the name of Jesus, Mary and Joseph were ye deein' there? Why didn't ye cover yer bits?' 'Well,' says the other, 'Aa divvent knaa aboot your parishioners. But mine, it's me face they'd reco'nise!'

AA COME TIV A COMPROMISE LIKE ....

HE WANTED BURIED AT SEA
AND AA WANTED HIM CREMATED

When Peggy's husband dies he wants his ashes scattered at the bingo at the Metro Centre. That way he reckons his wife and the girls'll visit at least twice a week.

Peggy went to the police station to keep Meggy company. 'Aa've come to report a missin' husband,' says Meggy. 'Oh, aye?' says the sergeant, 'Let's hev 'is description then.' 'Reet,' says Meggy, 'He's six foot two, slim, blonde, blue eyes, well spoken, well mannered...' Peggy nudges her and whispers, 'No, he's not! He's a baaldy little nowt with a beer gut!' 'Sssh!' says Meggy, 'Aa divvint want the same one back.'

Jonty took his young'un down the allotment last Sunday morning for a treat. Poor bairn was bored to tears and winged all day. When they got back home Jonty says to their lass, 'That's the last time! He's been such a naughty boy!' So the young'un says 'I wasn't naughty all the time. I was a good boy too.' 'When were you a good boy?' says Jonty. 'Must've been when you weren't lookin', Da.'

Jonty decided to improve himself. He bought a dictionary and learned three new words every day. By the end of the week no one in the Riveters could understand a word he said.

Dodgy Ray was on his way out the door and their lass shouts 'Huw, Dodger! Divvint forget, we need a new plug for the bath if yer passin' the hardware shop.' As it happened Dodger was passing the hardware shop so he popped in and asked for one. 'D'ye knaa what size it is?' says the gadgy serving on. 'Size?' says Dodger, 'Divvent ask me. Aa didn't even knaa we had an electric bath!'

The turn turned up at a club in Ashington last week. A three-piece band. They loaded their sound equipment onto the stage and asked the concert chairman 'Where's the mains?' 'It's oot the back next tiv the Ladies.'

Half an hour later the concert chairman knocked on the dressing room door. 'Can you gan on after the bingo? Five minutes?' The guitarist popped his head out and said 'Nee bother, we're just tunin' up.' 'Tunin' up?' says the concert chairman, 'You've knaan aboot this gig for two month!'

Dodger was telling Jonty he fancied going on that Winalot diet again. 'What's that, like?' 'Ah man, it's great,' says Dodger, 'Ye just carry a pocketful o' yon dog meal and ivvry time ye feel peckish ye hoy a bit in yer gob. Puts you off eatin' owt else. Aa lost fower stone. Mind, aa ended up in hospital.' Well Jonty says 'Wey that's not much cop if ye ended up in hospital.' 'Oh, it was nowt to do wi' the diet. Aa got hit by the bread van while aa was sniffin' a lamppost.'

Before that one he tried the Whisky diet. He lost three days.

HA YE SEEN LAST THORSDAY?

Jonty went into Bootses the chemist and says 'Wor lass wants some Para-summick-or-other. Aa cannot remember what it was.' The pharmacist says 'Para-something?' Jonty says 'Aye, Para-summick.' The pharmacist scratched his head, 'Was it paraquat?' Jonty thought for a bit, 'Aye, it might've been. Giz a bottle of that.' So the pharmacist gave him a bottle of paraquat and Jonty went on his way. The assistant in the shop who had overheard the transaction said sheepishly 'You divvint think it mighta been paracetamol he was wantin', do you?' 'Bugger!' says the pharmacist. Grabbing a bottle of paracetamol he leapt the counter and raced down the street after Jonty. He eventually caught up outside the pork shop and gasped 'Jonty, was it paracetamol you were after?' 'Aye!' says Jonty, 'That was it. What's the difference like?' So the pharmacist says 'Twenty-two pence please.'

At the committee meeting of the club, the treasurer spoke up and said 'The end of year accounts are all in and we've still got an overdraft of three hundred pounds. Does anyone have any idea what we can do about it?' The concert chairman suggested 'Why don't we donate it to the bairns' Christmas party?'

Wallace the Pollis pulled a lad over on the spine road last week. He'd been weaving all over the road. 'Have you been drinking, Sir?' 'Drinkin'? ...Hic! Aye. Sivinteen pints. Aa'm mortal.' So Wallace says 'Can I ask you to blow into this then please?' The driver says 'Why? Do you not believe iz like?'

Jonty was in Specsavers. The optician says 'Can you read what it says on the board?' Jonty says 'Bord? A cannot even see its cage.'

**....IF YOU CAN JUST GIVE 'IM TWO O' THEM
FOWER TIMES A DAY**

Two of the white cattle at Chillingham Castle were talking one day. 'Aa'm worried in case we get that mad cow disease me.' His mate says 'Divvint worry, man. It doesn't affect us whippets.'

What does a Cullercoats donkey get for his lunch? - An hour just like everyone else.

A bloke from Darras Hall got married and told his wife he wanted the whole house cleaned and a meal ready every night when he got home. The first night he came in and was pleased to see that everything was exactly as he wanted.

A bloke from Jesmond told his wife the same thing and for the first couple of nights he came in and saw she hadn't quite managed everything but by the weekend there was a meal on the table, the house was sparkling and she had even mown the lawn.

When Jonty got married he told his wife 'Nuw mind, every neet when I get in, aa want the place hoovered, beds made, ferrets cleaned oot, pigeons fed, fresh newspaper on the table, a hot meal and the top off a bottle of beer.' The first day he saw nothing. The second day he saw nothing. By the third day the swelling was going down and he could see out of one eye.

It was a quiet night at Newcastle airport. Two of the ground staff were playing cards. Duffy says 'Pity we've got nee beer to drink.' 'Aye,' says Biffa, 'There's nen left.' They had a hunt around but couldn't find anything. Even the sherry from Christmas was finished. 'Tell you what,' says Biffa, 'someone telt iz once that there's alcohol in aviation fuel.' Duffy says 'Wow! Wey we've plenty of that if you want to try it.' So they tried a little sip and it wasn't too bad. Then they had another few sips and started feeling a bit piddly-paddly. 'Hey, it's just the donkey's this, mind.' They spent the rest of the night playing cards and getting merry. It was the phone ringing that woke Biffa next morning. 'Huw, Biffa. Is that ye?' Biffa says 'Aye. Whe's that?' 'It's me, man. Are ye aallreet?' Biffa says 'Aye, champion. That was a canny bevvy we had last neet. Nee hangower neither.' Duffy says 'Aye it was darza. Aa've got nee hangower neither. Tell you what mind though but... Have you farted yet?' Biffa had to think, he says 'Er, nar. Not yet.' Duffy says 'Aye, well divvint. Aa'm at Gatwick me!'

When Davy Norris got divorced the judge says to him 'Mr Norris, having reviewed your wife's financial situation, I have decided to award her the sum of £450 per month.' Davy says 'Aye, champion. That's varry kind of ye, yer reverence. Aa'll try to bung her a few quid mesel' when aa can.'

Two nuns were driving home one night past Gosforth Park when a vampire stepped out in front of the car and they had to screech to a halt. 'What'll we dee?' says the young nun. 'Just show him yer cross!' So the young nun wound down the window and screamed 'Nick off! Or wuz'll get oot an' chin ye, ye goofy little nowt!'

Dodger got in the other night and flopped on the settee, 'Get iz a beer, Pet. Afore it starts.' His wife brought him a beer from the kitchen. He thanked her and knocked it back quickly. 'Can you get iz another one afore it starts, Pet.' His wife groaned and brought him another beer and banged it down in front of him. 'Thanks, Pet. Any chance o' puttin' the chip pan on, afore it starts?' Well, she came storming back through and starts shouting at him 'Na! There is nee chance. An' if you think aa'm ganna run back an' forth aall neet wi' beer an' scran while ye lie there an' dee nowt – after the day aa've had. Aa've been doon the launderette, up yer mother's, ower the toon ....' Dodger just sighed and said 'Whoa! Doesn't matter, Pet. It's started.'

Dodgy Ray's wife was ratching round in the pantry to find an onion to put in Dodger's corned beef sarny. The daft bugger found a daffodil bulb and chopped that up by mistake. Dodger ended up in hospital. They're keeping him in. But he'll be out in the spring.

A couple in their nineties queued up in the caff near the sea front in Blyth. When they got to the front they ordered one fish and chips between them. They sat at a table and as other customers looked on, the man cut the fish in half and then started counting the chips into two piles. Jonty was waiting in the queue and saw this and took pity. He offered to buy them a portion each as he'd won the domino the night before. They insisted that one was enough and they had always shared everything for the last 70 years. Then the old bloke tucked in while his wife looked on. She just sat there and lovingly watched every mouthful he took. Jonty went over again and says 'Yer chips'll be gettin' caad, pet. Get stuck in, man woman.' The old lady just smiled and says 'I cannot, Pet. It's his torn wi' the teeth.'

There was a collision between two wagons on the roundabout between Newbiggin and Ashington. One was carrying a cargo of tortoises and the other was transporting terrapins. Both wagons overturned and shed their loads. The BBC's Ashington correspondent reported it was a turtle disaster.

Two cows were watching the traffic going past on the A69. One says 'Moo!' and the other one says 'That's just what aa was ganna say.'

Dodger had a pal called one-arm Kev. He only had one arm. Otherwise he would've been called just Kev. 'Where you off to?' says Dodger when he saw him at the bus stand. 'Aa'm away to change a light bulb for me ma.' Dodger looked at him and his one arm '…Is that not difficult?' 'Na,' says Kev, 'Aa've got the receipt an'that.'

BUT FOLKS KEEP TRYIN' TO
STICK PENNIES IN ME HEED!

Dodgy Ray went into the Riveters one Saturday lunchtime 'Was aa in heor lastneet?' he says to the barman. 'Aye, aall neet, Dodger,' says the barman. 'Wey did aa spend a lot of money?' 'Must've been nigh-on thorty quid,' says the barman. Dodger was relieved, 'Thank Gawd fer that! Aa thowt aa'd gone and wasted it!'

There's a lad lives next door to Jonty that's not the full onion. Definitely not plumb. The wheel's going round but the hamster's dead. You know what I mean? He collects spiders and things in matchboxes. He was telling me one day he had a centipede for a friend. Aa says 'Oh, aye. Where is he then?' 'He's in me matchbox. We're gan doon the park to play football.' So he opened the box a little bit but nowt happened. We both waited. In the end I got sick so just for a laugh, I bent down and shouted 'Howway mister centipede. Come an' play football.' Just then a little voice from inside the box shouts 'Giz a chance to get me boots on, man!'

Betty Steed went into the office of the Gateshead Post to put an announcement in for her husband who'd just died. When she saw how much they charge per line she was shocked. She decided to keep it brief, so she filled in the slip and handed it over. It read 'Nobby Steed of Gatesheed's deed.' The lass behind the counter said 'There's room for another three words if you want.' So Betty wrote it out again. 'Nobby Steed of Gatesheed's deed. Cortina for sale.'

Dodger's eldest lad came to his dad for some advice. 'Fatha, Aa want to marry Donna cos she's me childhood sweetheart and she's geet lush an' aa love her loads.' So Dodger says 'That's champion son. What's the problem?' He says 'Wey there's this crabbity aad widow that fancies iz. And she's loaded and she sez she'll give iz a million pund if aa marry 'er. What would ye dee?' So Dodger says 'You must follow yer heart son. Marry the lass you love. It waddn't be fair otherwise.' He was happy with the advice and went off to propose to Donna. Just as he was leaving, Dodger shouts 'So er, where's this widow live then?'

Jonty's eldest lad, Young Jonty, was at a job interview. There was a posh bloke sitting next to him with an Oxford University tie on. He looked at Jonty and was amazed to see he was wearing the same tie. 'Excuse me,' says he, with a gob full of liggies, 'You don't look like the sort of person who would've been up to Oxford.' Young Jonty says 'Wey there you gan. Ye nivver can tell.' So the posh lad says 'Tell me, what did you do at Oxford?' So Young Jonty says 'Aa bowt mesel a new tie.'

Jonty went to the Shop Steward. He says 'Aa hear yer a great believer in free speech.' He says 'Aye, what's the problem?' Jonty says 'Lend iz yer phone, man.'

Dodger took his wife to Stowell Street for an anniversary meal. They were enjoying the main course when Dodger found a twig in his chow mein. 'Huw! Waiter!' he shouts 'There's a twig in me scran.' The waiter had a look and said 'Sorry, Sir. I'll fetch the branch manager immediately'

When Geordie won the pools and moved to Darras Hall one of his snobby neighbours came over for a bit natter. He says 'Course here in Ponteland we believe that breeding is far more important than wealth.' So Geordie says 'Ah, aye. It's pretty important in Blakelaw an'aall but we have loads of other interests besides.'

Two Geordie rules of life:
Number 1 - Divvent let on to people everything you know.
Number 2 - . . . .

When me Uncle Geordie went to live in London he used to bore the pants off the Cockneys by telling them what a wonderful place Newcastle is. Every night in the pub he'd be bragging about the beer, the women, the countryside, the coastline, the quayside etc. One night one of the cockneys got sick and says 'If it's so bleedin' wonderful how come you live down here then?' Geordie says 'Wey it's cos they're all so clivvor up there, I had to come doon here to stand a chance of mekkin it!'

AA DIVVENT MIND YE TRAININ' THE DOG...

BUT WHY YE USIN' ME MAM'S CARDY?

Famous Geordies

This could never be a comprehensive list as Geordies are becoming famous as we speak. It's a list compiled by asking people who they think should be included. Apologies if I didn't get round to asking you - or including you. Any omissions will be included in future editions. It's also difficult to list people in order of importance. The success of ex-models who marry ex-Beatles can never rank alongside the heroism of Lord Collingwood at Trafalgar, the inventions of the Stephensons or William Armstrong. So they're in alphabetical order.

There isn't enough room here to list all their credits but everyone on this list can be looked up on the internet for more information.

Sadly, those northeast personalities who have pledged allegiance to S*nd*rl*nd have been excluded. I'm sure one day they will appear on a list of famous Mackems. Probably on the back of a tab packet.

Admiral Lord Collingwood - Hero of Trafalgar,
Alan Hull - Singer/Songwriter,
Alan Plater - Writer, Alan Shearer - Footballer,
Albert Stubbins - Footballer,
Alex Glasgow - Writer, Andy Taylor - Musician,
Ant and Dec - Actors/TV Presenters,
Arthur Holmes - Geologist,
Baron Harry Woolf - Lord Chief Justice,
Baron Taylor of Gosforth - Lord Chief Justice,
Basil Bunting - Poet, Billy Fane - Actor/Comedian,
Bob Stokoe - Footballer, Bobby Charlton - Footballer,
Bobby Thompson - Comedian, Brendan Foster - Athlete,
Brian Ferry - Singer, Brian Johnson - Singer AC/DC,
Bruce Welch - Musician,

Capability Brown - Landscape Gardener,
Cardinal Basil Hume - Archbishop of Westminster,
Carol Malone - Journalist, Presenter,
Catherine Cookson - Writer,   Charles Palmer - Shipbuilder,
Charles Sheridan Swan - Shipbuilder,
Charlie Hardwick - Actor,   Chas Chandler - Musician/Manager,
Cheryl Tweedy - Singer,   Chris Waddle - Footballer,
Clair Rutter - Opera Singer,
Col. Jim Porter - Newcastle Brown Ale,
Dame Flora Robson - Actor,   Daniel Gooch - Politician,
David Scott Cowper - Yachtsman,   Denise Welch - Actress,
Derek Hare - Artist,
The Donald Brothers - VIZ Comic,
Donna Air - Actor, Presenter,   Emily Davies - Suffragette,
Emily Woof - Actor,   Eric Burdon - Singer,
Felicity Finch - Actor,   Geordie Ridley - Singer/Songwriter,
George Hunter - Shipbuilder,   George House - Broadcaster,
George Stephenson - Engineer,   Ginger Walls - Singer,
Grace Darling - Heroine,   Graham Radcliffe - Mountaineer,
Hank Marvin - Musician,   Harry Clasper - Rower,
Heather Mills - ex-model, ex-wife of Paul McCartney,
Hilton Valentine - Musician,
Howard Kendall - Football Manager,   Ian Le Frenais - Writer,
Jack Brymer - Musician,
Jack Charlton - Footballer,   Jackie Milburn - Footballer,
James Hill - Fiddle Player/Composer,
Janice Cairns - Soprano,   Jayne Middlemiss - Presenter,
Jill Halfpenny - Actor,   Jimmy Nail - Singer/Writer/Actor,
Joanne Conway - Skater,
Joe Wilson - Singer/Songwriter,   John Clayton - Town Clerk,
John Dobson - Architect,   John Marley - Civil War Hero,
John Gilroy - Commercial Artist,   Eric Idle - Monty Python,
John Martin - Artist,   John Nichol - Gulf War Hero,
John Simpson Kirkpatrick - Gallipoli Hero,

John Steel - Musician,   John Wilson Carmichael - Artist,
John Woodvine - Actor,   Johnny Handle - Singer/Musician,
Kevin Whateley - Actor,   Lawrie McMenemy - Footballer,
Lewis Fry Richardson - Inventor,   Libby Davison - Actor,
Michael Chaplin - Writer,   Michelle Heaton - Singer,
Mike McLeod - Athlete,   Mike Neville - Broadcaster,
Miriam Stoppard - Doctor/TV Personality,
Myles Birket Foster - Artist,   Neil Atkinson - Photographer
Neil Tennant - Singer,   Nick Brown - Politician,
Ove Arup - Engineer (Sydney Opera House, Byker Viaduct,)
Owen Brannigan - Classical Singer,
Paddy McAloon - Musician,   Paul Gascoingne - Footballer,
Paul Smith - Singer,   Peter Beardsley - Footballer,
Ray Kennedy - Footballer,   Richard Grainger - Architect,
Ridley Scott - Film Director,
Robert Stephenson - Engineer,
Robson Green - Actor,   Rosie Rowell - Actor,
Ross Noble - Comedian,   Rowan Atkinson - Actor,
Simon King - Hairy Biker
Sheila Armstrong - Opera Singer,   Sid Chaplin - Writer,
Sid Waddell - Commentator,   Sir John Hall - Entrepreneur,
Sir Thomas Allen - Opera Singer,   Steve Bruce - Footballer,
Steve Harmison - Cricketer,   Sting - Musician,
Steve Watson - Footballer,   Thomas Bewick - Artist/Engraver,
Thomas Burt - Politician,   Tim Healy - Actor,
Timothy Hackworth - Engineer,   Tod Slaughter - Actor,
Tom Graveney - Cricketer,
Tom Hadaway - Writer,   Tom McConville - Musician,
Tommy Armstrong - Writer/Singer,   Val McLane - Actor
Venerable Bede - Christian Scholar/Historian,
Wee Georgie Wood - Entertainer,
William Armstrong - Engineer,   Arthur Holmes - Geologist,
William Hedley - Engineer,   William Shield - Composer
And three of the Baghdaddies Band

Constitutional Amendments

The right to speak the native tongue of Geordieland
whatever the company - even in Jesmond.

The right to bare arms and legs in the Bigg Market
and Quayside areas during winter months.

The right to wear a Toon top to all functions.

The right to talk to strangers throughout the world
and brag about Newcastle upon Tyne
and surrounding areas.

The right for a man to have a tab outside Tescos
while their lass does the shopping.

The right to wear a cap at all times
-except when it's raining.
(Ye divvent want to sit in the hoose wi' a wet cap)

The right for man to drive to a function
and his wife to drive home - now and then.

The right for a man to do the dishes without
their lass lettin' on to his mates.

Geordie Quiz

Score over 130 - Geet clivvor like owt
100 - 130 - Canny clivvor
80 - 99 - Ye'll dee
60 - 79 - Not ower clivvor
Under 60 - Ye divven' knaa nowt ye!

1. What was the full original name of the massive Government office complex on Benton Park Road?

2. Which listed building on Claremont Road was once a Golf Club?

3. Name the motorcycle shop that was nextdoor to the Haymarket bus station.

4. Which drink was produced at Prudhoe Place?

5. Which nightclub was nextdoor to the Mayfair?

6. Where in Newcastle could you watch non-stop cartoons on a Saturday morning?

7. Which famous Geordie Dame had a Newcastle playhouse named after her?

8. Where was it?

9. Where was the Toddle Inn Café?

10. A cinema on Shields Road and one on Two Ball Lonnen had the same name. What was it?

11. Which Tyneside duo had hits including 'Let's Get Ready to Rumble'?

12. Which Tyneside vocalist has helped her all-girl band to several UK hits?

13. Which Tyneside vocalist took his duo to a UK Christmas number one?

14. Who was the only Geordie footballer in the 2006 England World Cup Squad?

15. Which hot food takeaway was the nearest to the Haymarket Cinema?

16. Which 'Bridge' leading to the Haymarket is no longer a bridge but still keeps the name?

17. Which park lost its paddling pool to make way for the central Motorway?

18. Which beautiful building on New Bridge Street was demolished in the 60s to make way for a hideous concrete monstrosity - demolished in 2007?

19. Which notorious council leader was responsible for the demolition of several beautiful buildings in his quest to make Newcastle a city of the future?

20. Which Coronation Street grocer was thrown from a multi-storey car park in the cult movie 'Get Carter'?

21. Before de-regulation, Newcastle's famous yellow buses shared the streets with which 'Red Bus' company?

22. Which Newcastle school was officially opened the same day as the new Tyne Bridge?

23. What was the original name of the ferry which became the Tuxedo Princess?

24. Which road would you walk down from the Central Station to the Black Gate?

25. The church on the corner of Newgate Street and Gallowgate inspired the brand name of which product?

26. In 1878, The landlord of the Duke of Wellington died, aged 22. Why did his funeral procession attract a crowd of over thirty thousand?

27. Which department store on Shields Road had its own credit system and currency?

28. Which locally famous surgeon, celebrated in song, was based at the Forth Infirmary - Near the Central Station?

29. Which Newcastle department store was 'Never knowingly undersold'?

30. What was the trade of David Haggie, Mayor of Gateshead in 1854?

31. Which much sought after brand of Tyneside pottery products were made at the largest pottery in Britain and possibly the world?

32. Thomas Burt was the first pitman to become what?

33. Which famous soap-star window cleaner attended St Cuthberts school in Newcastle?

34. Name the cycle shop that stood on the right of Handyside's Arcade entrance.

35. Which naval officer whose monument overlooks the Tyne, was born in Side in 1748?

36. Which two Tyne bridges are joined together?

37. Which Tyne bridge is nearest to the site of the first ever Newcastle/Gateshead bridge?

38. Which historic building originally stood between Cloth Market and Groat Market?

39. Where was the Tyneside Irish Centre before it moved to China Town?

40. Which Tyneside Poet was born on Stowell Street?

41. Is the Blaydon Races song a true story?

42. Which three Geordie sisters made 'Dance To Your Daddy' famous?

43. Which regular member of the 'Rising Damp' cast was brought up in Newcastle and attended St Cuthbert's School?

44. The biggest covered market in the country, containing 243 shops, was built in 1835. What was it called?

45. Which Newcastle venue has hosted live performances by Rachmaninov, Strauss, Liszt and even Charles Dickens?

46. In which year was the Great Fire? 1694, 1762 or 1854?

47. What did Charles Parsons build in 1894 to demonstrate his new steam turbine?

48. Which two brothers played for Newcastle in the FA Cup winning team of 1952?

49. What was unusual about the presentation of the cup that year?

50. Which famous landscape gardener was from Geordieland?

51. Which Team has Newcastle beaten twice in FA Cup finals?

52. Who lost his head in 1941 and got it back in 1947?

53. Which prestige furniture manufacturer had his showroom on the corner of Jesmond Road and The Great North Road before the new Central Motorway forced a move?

54. Which Tyneside father and son were instrumental in the development of rail travel throughout the world?

55. Which building was the first in Britain to utilise curved wrought iron ribs to hold its enormous roof?

56. Which sport was carried out on the roadway of the High Level Bridge in the 1850s?

57. Where in Newcastle is there a monument to the war in South Africa?

58. Which Geordie actor played the part of Inspector Witty in Z Cars?

59. Which Geordie actress played the part of DC and later DS Rawton in The Bill?

60. Which Geordie actress plays Val in Emmerdale?

61. Which Geordie actor started as a porter in Casualty?

62. Which actress played the first Geordie landlady of The Rover's Return?

63. Which Geordie actor played the part of Spender's pal Stick?

64. Which Longbenton footballer had two spells at Newcastle and achieved 59 England Caps?

65. Which Gateshead footballer played for Newcastle, Spurs, Lazio etc., and achieved 57 England Caps?

66. Which Czech goalkeeper does the Toon Army regularly reassure that he IS a Geordie?

67. Which Byker Grove actress became a presenter on the Big Breakfast and MTV?

68. Which regular Byker Grove actor had a column in the Evening Chronicle and was voted Club Comedian of the Year?

69. Which Geordie actress appeared in both Eastenders and Coronation Street and is quite a canny dancer too?

70. Which famous locomotive ended up on its side after being de-railed by striking miners?

71. What was the Crooked Billet?

72. Which Geordie boxer was Mike Tyson's sparring partner?

73. Which member of the Royal family opened the Gateshead International Garden Festival in 1990?

74. Which Newcastle market was the regular location for the informal 'Paddy's Market'?

75. A monument to which famous Geordie stands at the junction of Westgate Road and Neville Street?

76. Which Geordie lass presented Top Of The Pops and The O Zone?

77. Who played for Newcastle United and Gateshead and went on to manage Northern Ireland?

78. Which sportsman had his funeral at St Nicholas Cathedral and his ashes scattered at the Gallowgate End?

79. Tyneside guitarist Andy Taylor helped which band to several UK hits?

80. Which road takes you from Gallowgate to Grey's Monument?

81. What was Grey Street originally named?

82. What was introduced at Wembley in 1924 to cope with Newcastle's popularity?

83. What was Newcastle's Albert Shepherd the first person to do at an FA Cup Final?

84. When it was launched in 1906 it was the biggest, luxury passenger liner ever built on the Tyne. What was its name?

85. Where in the North-East was the first Ark Royal aircraft carrier built?

86. Where did AMC hold their first-ever British drive-in movie?

87. Give the second names to the following Tyneside industrial partnerships: Hawthorn …., Armstrong…., Swan…, Vickers…, Wigham …..

88. Which Tyneside instrumental band had their first UK no1 in 1960?

89. Which Tyneside harmony group had a UK number one hit with 'After the Goldrush'?

90. Which Tyneside rock band had a UK number one hit in 1964?

91. Which historic building stood opposite the church on Gallowgate until 1978 when it became a car park?

92. What was Rosie's bar called while Rosie was in charge?

93. Which venue once staged boxing six nights a week?

94. Where's this roof?

95. And this one?

96. And this one?

97. And this one?

98. And finally, this one?

99. Which city centre street is this?

100. And this one?

101. What was this building for many years?

102. Which street is this?

103. Which Street is this?

104. Which Tyneside singer/musician took his group to several UK number ones including 'Message in a Bottle'?

105. Which Dunston-born singer left 'Geordie' to join AC-DC?

106. Which Tyneside actor/singer had many UK hits including 'Love Don't Live Here Any More'?

107. Which Tyneside band had many UK hits including Lady Eleanor?

108 Which Scottish born singer/guitarist, brought up in Newcastle, is responsible for the 'Local Hero' theme tune 'Going Home?'

109. Which Teetotaller opened Newcastle's first coffee shop in the Cloth Market? The building still bears his name but ironically, the coffee shop is now a pub!

110. Why is The Hoppings held on Newcastle Town Moor during race week?

111. Which company had a cigarette factory on the New Coast Road?

112. Which Newcastle building was conceived and built by a bass player and a sax player?

113. Name the Cinema that was next to the fire station on Gosforth High Street

114. Which Newcastle park is this?

115. In which city centre park is this lake?

116. And where is this lake

117. This is Birdcage walk. In which park is it?

118. Where on the Ouseburn is this bridge?

119. Where is this Peace garden?

120. Where on Tyneside is this park?

121. Which road takes you from the Royal Victoria Infirmary's original main gate to the Haymarket?

122. On which road is Newcastle Speedway?

123. Which structure was removed from the Exhibition Park shortly after the exhibition?

124. Where was Newcastle's College of Science and Technology, later The College of Further Education, affectionately known as 'The College of Knowledge'?

125. Where is this Tyne bridge?

126. Where is this Tyne bridge?

127. Where do these bridges cross the Tyne?

128. Where does this bridge cross the Tyne?

129. For which sport was Harry Clasper famous?

130. Who was the Newcastle captain and goalscorer when Newcastle won the 1969 Fairs Cup?

131. On which Newcastle street would you find The Bacchus?

132. On which street would you find the Blackie Boy?

133. Which whisky was made under Byker Bridge?

134. And which brand of bleach was made nearby?

135. What accolade was awarded Newcastle by the Reader's Digest in 2005?

136. Which accolade did BBC Radio 4 listeners award to Grey Street?

137. Alongside which river is Red Walk?

138. Where in Newcastle is there a cluster of street names inspired by Shakespeare?

139. Where is the unlikely named Orchard Street?

140. Which riverside road leads from Forth Banks to Water Street?

141. Which road passes through the Chinese Arch?

142. What happened to Mark Sherwood at Gallowgate in 1844?

143. When Edward Baily finished building Grey's Monument, what did he build next?

144. Which Methodist Church stands on a medieval lane leading to Northumberland Street?

145. Which North East actor/comedian was part of the 'Not The Nine o'Clock News' team?

146. Which pub is in the Central Station?

147. What's the popular name for The Market Lane Pub?

148. Is Hadrian's Wall 63, 69, 73 or 76 miles long?

149. Which city centre landmark did King Olav of Norway officially open in 1968?

150. What was built in 1842 to transport coal through the city to the Tyne?

Answers on Page 182

Geordie Rhyming Slang

Six an ites – Straights
Yer gannin' six an' ites but?

Corned Beef
Deaf – hard of hearing

Jekkyls
Jekkyl and Hydes – Strides (Trousers)
'Ees flyin' 'is jekkyls at haff mast'

Harry Tait
Bait

Dolly Dimple – Simple

Orson
'Orse n' cart – Shart.
Aa've gettn kebab saace aallower me orson

Broon Breed
Deed – Dead

Leazers
Leazes Park – Dark
It's a bit leazers in here

Hank Marvin – Starving

Spuggy's – Spuggy's nest – Chest

Tyneside Firsts

World's **First** use of the term 'English' – Venerable Bede

World's **First** reinforced concrete – William Wilkinson

World's **First** electric light switch – John Henry Holmes

MEBBE'S THIS IS IT?

World's **First** light bulb factory was in Benwell

World's **First** house to be lit by electricity – Cragside Hall

World's **First** transparent sticking plaster – John Morrison

World's **First** iron built steam collier – Charles Mark Palmer

World's **First** artificial liver – Newcastle University

World's **First** police chase in a motor car

The **First** 1000-year record of annual rainfall
– Newcastle University

World's **First** turbine generator – Charles Parsons

World's **First** 'Plasticine' – William Harbutt

World's **First** windscreen wiper – Gladstone Adams

World's **First** hydraulic crane – William Armstrong

World's **First** purpose-built lifeboat – William Wouldhave

World's **First** tilting bridge – Gateshead Millenium

The **First** coal port in the world – Newcastle

World's **First** combined road and rail bridge – The High Level

The **First** Rolls Royce bonnet mascot 'The Spirit of Ecstasy'
Designed by Charles Robinson Sykes

World's **First** street lit by gas – Mosely Street

World's **First** street lit by electricity – Mosely Street

World's **First** production of Domestos, Fairy Soap and Liquid, Be-Ro, Andrews and Lucozade

The **First** dog show in the world

The **First** beauty contest in Britain – Olympia Theatre

World's **First** hydro-electric power system – Cragside

World's **First** kipper was smoked at Seahouses

World's **First** purpose-built locomotive factory – Robert Stephenson & Co. Forth Banks

World's **First** department store – Bainbridge's

The **First** Briton to conquer Everest by the north and the south routes – Graham Radcliffe

World's **First** flavoured potato crisp – Hoggets

The **First** locomotive for the USA – Stephenson's Works

The **First** locomotive for Germany – Stephenson's Works

World's **First** Trilby hat – Fenwick

The **First** light rapid-transit system in the country – The Tyne and Wear Metro

The **First** history of the English people – Venerable Bede

The **First** to break the French line and open fire at Trafalgar – Admiral Collingwood

World's **First** breech-loader artillery gun – Armstrong's

The **First** British team to clone a human embryo
– Newcastle University

World's **First** use of AD and BC dates – Venerable Bede

World's **First** locomotive passenger coach – John Atkinson

SORRY, PET. IT'S NOT DUE TILL 1825

Big Things!

Newcastle was once Britain's **biggest** pottery supplier
and Maling was the country's biggest pottery

The Central Station's diamond crossing was
the **biggest** in the world

The Tyne was Britain's **biggest** coal exporter

The Tyne Bridge was the world's **biggest** single span bridge

The **biggest** sculpture in Britain is the Angel of the North

Scottish & Newcastle is the country's **biggest** brewer

Europe's **biggest** out-of-town shopping complex is the
Metro Centre in Gateshead

The world's **biggest** half-marathon is the Great North Run

The Hoppings is the world's **biggest** travelling fairground

The Ministry at Benton was the **biggest** office
complex in Britain.
In the western world only the Pentagon was bigger!

Britain's **biggest** man-made lake is Kielder

The **biggest** wooden structure in Europe – Dunston Staithes

UK's **biggest** door-to-door tea delivery company – Ringtons

Norwegian Geordie

There are many Norwegian words that have been adopted into the English language and vice-versa but what is interesting about this list is the pronunciation of words which are commonly used in the north east.

Norse	Geordie	English
Barn	Bairn	Child
Beit	Bait	Food
Bluse	Bloose	Blouse
Brekke	Brek	Break
Cracian	Crack	Banter
Flytte	Flit	Move
Genser	Ganzie	Sweater
Gi	Gi	Give
Hjem	Hyem	Home
Hus	Hoose	House
Kista	Kist	Tool box, chest
Kitla	Kittle	Tickle
Klaer	Claes	Clothes
Krakk	Crackett	Stool
Lasqar	Lass	Girl
Nei	Nee	No
Poki	Poke	Bag, pouch, pocket
Rundt	Rund	Around
Skita	Skitters	Diarrhoea
Skjørt	Skort	Skirt
Skjorte	Short	Shirt
Strangr	Strang	Strong
Ute	Oot	Out

WEY IT WAS YE THAT SHOOTED FOR A NORSE!

Medical Terms

Kincough
Whooping cough

Snottysneck
Common cold

Stottinheed
Headache

Oot o' lamp oil
Poor sight

Bad wi' the beor
Hangover

Gettn' the smitt
Becoming infected

Cannaswallie
Sore throat

Not ower clivvor
General malaise

Skitters
Diarrhoea

Ootablaah
Breathless

An arse like a mackem rosette
Inflamed haemorrhoids

AARGH NAR!!. . . .

AA'M GETTN A SPOT!!

Lazyitis
Tired

Dart in th'heed
Sports injury

Divvent Gan Changin'
Another *fairly* Truthful Tale

Ruby Ruddick was doon on her hunkers
Givin' her front step a bit of a scrubbin'
While Leonard, her lodger, was in the netty oot back
Givin' 'is boots a good claggin' wi dubbin

Ruby shouted 'Good mornin', to folks waalkin' past
Didn't have to look up, knew their boots
But the mornin' in question, she seen a posh pair of brogues
Attached to some legs in a suit

And there stood this bloke, flashy tie, bowler hat
'I'm from London,' he says. She says 'So?
That's not my fault, are you wantin' a medal?'
He says 'I'm from Littlewoods Pools.' She says 'Oh.'

He says 'Besides, it's not you, it's your lodger I want.'
'Just my luck,' says poor Rube 'You might know.'
She dropped her brush in her pail and got up off her knees
She says 'Come through then.' So the bloke says 'Right-o.'

He followed her in doon the lobby and through to the back
'Who is it? Sod off!' shoots the budgie
She showed him through the back scullery oot into the yard
And she knocked on the door of the cludgie.

Leonard shoots 'Are you borstin? Just give iz a mo.'
But the bloke just gans 'No, take your time,
You've won half a million on Littlewoods Pools,
On account of eight draws on one line.

Well Leonard jumped up, he thowt 'What?' he says 'Eh?'
Divvent think he quite understood fully
All beside himself like, clashed 'is heed on 'is bike
That was hangin' in there on a pulley

He oppened the door, had a look at the cheque
And started to dee this bit dance
Sez the bloke 'I'll shake hands when you've washed 'em,
But first you'd best pull up your pants.'

137

'Said nowt about this in 'is horoscope last neet,'
Said Ruby gannin' quite faint
But bein' a reglar chorchganner
She said 'Thank you, oh Lord. Yer a saint.'

Leonard thowt he'd splash oot like he'd not done before
And he looked at the Littlewoods' feller
'That's the new me,' he thowt, and went straight out and bowt
A new suit, bowler hat an' umbrella

He blew seven and six in the Dicken's Tea Rooms
Pot of tea and two sausage rolls
Then he went for a haircut at a barber's, that posh
It nivvor had any red and white pole

'Would sir like a nice cut and a blow dry?'
Said the toffee-nosed barber geet smugly
He says 'Gan on then, son, but d'you think while you're on,
You can dee owt 'boot iz bein' so ugly?'

'Well actually,' says the bloke 'There's a clinic upstairs,
Does facelifts and stuff while-you-wait,
They could reshape your nose and straighten that chin.'
And Leonard thowt 'That would be great.'

He got 'is hair done aall posh then he toddled upstairs
And this bloke helped him pick a new nose
Then he put him to sleep and fitted it on
Alang with two lugs what he'd chose

So Leonard took lodgins for a couple of days
An' by the thord day, reet enough, looked just super
He looked better by far, like a real filum star
'Fact he looked just like what's-'is-name Cooper

He went to see Ruby she was swillin' her step
Faffin' on like an owld mother hen
And 'is horoscope had said summat aboot chorch bells
So he proposed to her reet there and then

She was aall owercome when he got doon on one knee
Cos her step was still wet like as not
He says 'You don't look ower good but you do canny leek puds,
Should wuz gan an' get wed then, or what?'

She'd never seen him behave so romantic afore
But she agreed and said 'Aye. Might as well.'
So they went rund to speak to the Parson
He was up a height, fixin' one of 'is bells

He shoots doon 'Alreet, pet?' to Ruby
But as he did he let gan o' the rope
And a two-ton bell landed on Leonard
That just shows divvent trust horoscopes

Leonard never had a clue and then when he come to
He saw two pearly gates and felt sick
And Ruby went spare that neet sayin' a prayer
She says 'God, that was a reet dorty trick.'

As usual, not expectin' an answer from God
So she nearly dropped deed when he spoke
He says 'What's the to-do, was it someone you knew?'
She says 'Aye, man. It was Leonard. Me bloke.'

He says 'Len?' she says 'Aye!' 'In a suit and a tie?
It didn't look nowt like him,' said God
'All them fancy new clothes, new lugs and new nose,
I didn't knaa it was him, the daft sod!'

Recipes For Some Canny Bait

Here's some of the scran I prepare quite often myself. I'm no chef so the ideas, based on traditional recipes, have been adapted so they can be cooked in the modern kitchen using ingredients available at your local Co-op or corner shop.

They're easy enough for blokes living on their own. Some chefs may shake their heads at the use of stock cubes and other conveniences but hey, there's nee snobs here!

Drop Scones

There's nothing specifically Geordie about this recipe but Tyneside seems to be one of the few places that serves them fried with a full English breakfast. Heat them through in the pan after the sausage, bacon and black pudding have left a tasty residue.

Otherwise add sugar instead of the mustard and perhaps a dash or two of lemon essence and have them buttered with jam or honey.

Ingredients to serve four:
Half a pound of self-raising flour
Not quite half a teaspoon of salt
Half a teaspoon of dried mustard
1 egg
Half a pint of milk
A bit of butter

Sieve the flour into a mixing bowl and add the mustard powder and salt.

Beat the egg in a jug with half of the milk and add it to the bowl. Mix till it's smooth then add more milk until you have a batter a bit thicker than pancake batter.

Grease a heavy frying pan with the butter and heat it up. Using a desert spoon, drop a few dollops in the pan leaving space between for them to spread.

After a couple of minutes you'll see see bubbles on the surface, carefully turn them over and cook the other side until they're golden. If you're eating them straight away, wrap in a teatowel to keep warm and save drying out.

AA'VE PLUCKED IT AND STUFFED IT
BUT YE'LL HA' TO KILL IT!

Kipper Kedgeree

This is a recipe brought back by our lads serving in India and adapted to suit the Tyneside palate. It was originally a breakfast dish but makes a great lunch or evening meal. The fish must be smoked but you can use kipper, cod, mackerel or haddock. It should be cooked and flaked removing all the bones. If you use whole kippers fry them long enough for the bones to become brittle and edible but still remove as many as you can.

Ingredients to serve 2:
About 12 ounces of fish (Two small kippers, kipper fillets, smoked cod or haddock etc)
2 hard boiled eggs - chopped
1 mug of long grain rice – washed and left to dry
1 level teaspoon of turmeric
1 medium onion finely chopped
A few mushrooms
Red or green pepper or both
1 pint of chicken or vegetable stock
Olive oil and butter

Melt a little butter in a large frying pan and add a little olive oil. Add the onions and turmeric and fry lightly until soft. Add the mushrooms and peppers and keep turning the mixture to ensure even colouring. Add the rice and cook very gently until the grains start to look clear instead of white. Add the stock, bring it to the boil, reduce the heat and simmer until the rice has absorbed the stock but still remains quite firm. Don't let it go stodgy. Pour off some liquid if there's too much. When the rice is firm but cooked, add the fish and the eggs. Gently fold together and serve immediately in bowls with a knob of butter. (Or mayonnaise if you live in Jesmond.)

Stuffed Tetties

Make as many as you like. This recipe serves one – just experiment with the ingredients. There's no rules!

Ingredients to serve one greedy nowt:
1 large potato
Half an onion
A bit butter
A bit cheese
Whatever else you've got spare in the fridge
Salt and pepper

Wash your potato, prog it all over with a fork. Rub butter or olive oil into the skin and while it's still claggy rub salt into it (that posh rock salt's the best.) Put it in a hot oven 200°c (400f Gas 6) for about an hour till it feels soft when you squeeze it -use the oven glove mind, divvent born yersel! If you want to bake it in a microwave, just prepare it the same way and cook on full power till it's soft. Then put it in the proper oven for 5 minutes to crisp up the skin so it looks right.

Let it cool enough to handle and then cut it in half lengthways. Scoop out the insides and plonk them in a big bowl. Make sure not to damage the skins.

Chop up the onion and heat it in a pan with butter or olive oil till it's soft. Now here's where you can hunt round the pantry for some other bits and pieces. Chop up some bacon, a few mushrooms, maybe a bit of red or green pepper for colour, tomato – owt you fancy. Go on, be adventurous. I like to crumble a bit of a lamb stock cube into the juice. You can use veggie cubes if you're that way inclined. Season it with black pepper or a tiny smidge of cayenne if you're up for it.

When that lot's softened put it in the bowl with the potato and gently mix it all together. Try to leave some lumps in to add some texture.

Now scoop it back into the skins and sprinkle cheese on top. At this stage you can cover them and refrigerate till later or even freeze them. If you're starving though, put them back in the oven at about 200°c (400f Gas 6) until they're heated through, the cheese is melted and starting to brown.

These are great for parties. They can be made well in advance and kept in one of them plastic ice cream boxes or Tupperware if you're posh. Just heat through and brown them when needed.

**SORRY, PET. AA WAS WATCHIN'
READY STEADY COOK AND...**

...AA FORGOT TO MEK YER DINNER

Lentil and Oat Broth

Here's another recipe that you can muck about with. Again there's no rules! You can freeze it too.

Ingredients:
Bacon bits, a ham shank, a bacon knuckle or just a few slices of bacon chopped up.
1 medium onion chopped up as fine as you can
2 big carrots finely grated
1 mugful of lentils – rinsed in cold water
2 potatoes chopped into little cubes
2-3 tablespoons of oats (porridge will do)
Stock from cooking the ham shank or a couple of stock cubes.

Boil the shank or knuckle in a large pan until it's cooked through. Keep the stock and chop up the lean bits of meat and put them back in the pan with the onions.

If you're using bacon bits or chopped up slices, fry them with the onions in the pan. You might need a little olive oil if the bacon is lean. Otherwise heat and soften the onions in olive oil for five minutes then add your bacon bits.

Once the onion's soft and the meat is heated, add a couple of pints of stock and heat it while you're grating the carrots. Use the finest setting on your grater. Add the grated carrots and the lentils then peel your potato and chop it into small cubes. Add the potato and oats; make sure it comes back to the boil. Once it's boiled, turn the gas down and let it simmer for a while with the lid on giving it a stir now and then and making sure it's not sticking to the bottom.

The soup is ready when the lentils have totally softened and almost disappeared into a nice creamy consistency. Use your potato masher in the pan and mash up what's left of the potato till there's no lumps. You can use a food processer, blender or electric whisk for this if you can be bothered cleaning it afterwards.

You can add cream and a sprig of parsley if you live in Jesmond. Serve with buttered stottie.

Bread and Butter Pudding

You can use plain white bread with the crusts on or off and it doesn't matter if it's yesterday's bread.

Ingredients to serve four:
6 slices of bread
Butter
Marmalade
Half a mug of sultanas
2 ounces of sugar
2 Eggs
1 pint of milk – Not that skimmed stuff mind!

Spread the bread with plenty of butter and a bit of marmalade.

Cut it into triangles and arrange them in a greased, ovenproof dish with the points sticking up (My pal Carol uses chocolate spread!)

Sprinkle on the sultanas and some of the sugar

Beat the eggs and milk together and pour them over the bread making sure every slice gets soaked.

Let this stand for about 20-30 minutes until the bread absorbs some of the milk.

Bake in the oven at 160°c (325f, Gas 3) for up to an hour or until set and the top is golden brown.

Easy Pease Puddin

There's a lot of recipes for pease pudding involving hours of preparation, muslin bags and stock pots. This recipe cuts a few corners - but it's quite a precise art so you may need to practise. Boil the peas separately using no salt or stock as it delays the softening process.

Ingredients:
1 medium onion
1 mug of Yellow split peas
1 small potato finely chopped or grated
Cooked bacon or ham chopped finely
Ham stock (A cube will do)
Butter or olive oil

You might have to soak the split peas – check the packet. Rinse and boil them in enough water to cover.

Soften the onions in a saucepan with butter or olive oil and add the finely chopped bacon or ham. Add the finely chopped potato and a pint of ham stock. Bring to the boil.

Keep an eye on the peas and when they're soft, drain them and add them to your stock. Now this is the quick recipe so you have to stand over the pot. Keep it on quite a high heat so that the stock is reducing all the time. Stir so it doesn't stick. You're waiting for the peas to totally disappear into a cream. If it looks like it's getting too dry too early, add more stock to keep it bubbling. It's better to have it slightly on the sloppy side because it will thicken up as it sets. When you're happy with the consistency pour it out into a bowl to set. When it's cool you should be able to turn it out, slice it and spread it. You may have to experiment to get the consistency right.

Serve with ham in a stottie – or with a smoked ham salad if you live in Darras Hall.

Beef Pitsockles

I read a version of this recipe in the Newcastle Journal whilst recovering in hospital following a motorbike accident. With my jaws wired together for the next six weeks and being fed several variations of chicken soup through a straw, I longed to try out this recipe. Having said that, just a bacon sarnie would've been bliss!

Ingredients to serve 4:
A pound and a half of stewing steak cut into cubes
2 sausages chopped into half inch pieces
1 big onion – chopped
2 carrots – chopped or sliced
Some plain flour
Half a pint of beef stock
Half a bottle of Newcastle Brown Ale (You can drink the rest)
Mushrooms
1 cup full of fresh cockles - not the ones in vinegar!
Salt and pepper
Butter and olive oil

Pre heat the oven to 200°c

Put the beef and sausage in a bowl. Season with salt and pepper and add a bit flour. Get your hands in and mix it till the meat is nicely coated.

Heat a knob of butter and a little olive oil in a pan and fry the coated beef and sausage until it starts to brown. Keep it moving. Don't worry if the pan gets a bit claggy in the process. Transfer the beef to a plate. Add the onion, carrot, and a bit more butter to the pan and fry till the onion is soft.

Put the meat back in and add beef stock and beer, stirring to mix in any gundge left by the flour etc. Pour the whole lot into the casserole dish.

Make sure the casserole lid fits tightly and place in the hot oven and cook for half an hour at 200°c (400f, Gas 6) then reduce the heat to 150°c (300f, Gas 2)

After another hour add the mushrooms. Check there is enough fluid, if not add some more stock.

Continue to cook for another half hour or until the meat is tender. Add the cockles and heat through just before serving so as not to overcook them. If the sauce is too watery it can be thickened by stirring in cornflour (mixed with cold water) and popped back in the oven for a few minutes. Or just mop up the extra gravy with a bit of stottie.

Serve with new potatoes and spring cabbage – or asparagus if you live in Stocksfield.

HUW! CAN YE SMELL CARROTS?

Stottie Cake

Although you can buy perfectly good stotties from Greggs or a decent bakery, no Geordie recipe list would be complete without our very own bread recipe. They're quite a tricky thing to make so you may need to practise before you invite guests to a stottie party. Here's how me mam used to make them. Make sure your working area is warm with no draughts. Mam used to lock the back door and hide the key so we couldn't run in and out. She did the same when making Yorkshire puddings.

Ingredients:
1lb strong plain breadmaking flour
1 level teaspoon of salt
2 oz. butter or margarine (you can experiment with olive oil too)
1 oz fresh yeast or 2 level teaspoons of dried
1 tsp. sugar (important to activate the yeast)
Quarter of a pint tepid water (not cold but not ower hot either!)
Quarter of a pint tepid milk

Mix together the flour and salt then rub in the butter.

In a small cup mix the yeast and sugar with some of the warm water. Stir and leave until the yeast dissolves and froths a bit.

Make a hole in the flour, add the yeast mixture and the rest of the water and milk. Mix it with your hands working into a firm dough that leaves the bowl clean.

Knead the dough on a floured board for about ten minutes. Sprinkle on a bit more flour if you think the dough's a bit soft.

Put the dough in a large lightly greased dish and cover with teatowels making sure no draughts can get in. Leave it to rise in a warm kitchen until it has doubled in size - probably an hour or more. A large plastic bag is good for this job too.

When it has risen put it back on the floured board and knead lightly to let out any air and to make the dough pliable again.

Separate into two pieces and roll them into round cakes about ¾ inch thick. Put them on a greased baking tray, sprinkle with flour, cover with the teatowel again and wait till they rise again. When they're twice the size, prog the middle with your finger to leave a hole. You can also stick a fork in a couple of places if you wish.

Place them in the oven just above halfway up. Bake at 200°c (400f, Gas 6) for 12 to 15 minutes. Turn them over near the end of cooking. You'll know they're ready if you can prog them with a fork and it comes out clean or my mam's method was to knock on the bottom with your knuckle: if it's quiet they're not done – if there's a definite 'knock' they're ready.

Singin' Hinnies

Not something that's made very often nowadays but a 'must' for any Geordie recipe book. You'll need a very heavy-based frying pan but a smooth griddle is better. These should really be eaten hot with butter, jam or honey so freeze any that you won't use before cooking – separate them with cling film or greaseproof paper. Have a party in your kitchen and eat them as they're cooked.

Ingredients to make half a dozen:
8 oz plain flour
1 teaspoon baking powder
4 oz best butter – very cold
Third of a pint of milk
Half a cup of sultanas or currants
Pinch of salt

Sift the flour into a mixing bowl and stir in the baking powder and salt. Add the butter and mix so that there are still quite a few tiny lumps of unmelted butter left in the mix.

Add the fruit and pour in the milk. Mix it until it's quite a firm dough.

On a floured board, roll the dough into a sausage shape and cut into 6 equal portions. Roll each of these into a thin scone.

Grease a very hot pan or griddle with a little butter and cook the scones for a few minutes, turning now and then to make sure they're evenly cooked and golden. Listen to them sing as the tiny pieces of butter burst into life!

AA TEK IT YUZ DIVVENT LIKE ME SCONES THEN?

Old Tyneside Songs

The words for the first song 'Where-ivver Ye Gan...' are taken from an original signed manuscript given by the composer Jack Robson to Stan Pearson of Morpeth when Stan sang on the 'Wotcheor Geordie' radio show.

The words for the other songs are mainly from memory and are the versions that have been handed down through the oral tradition for years, so there may be a few modifications to the original texts.

Where-ivver Ye Gan,
Yor Sure To Find A Geordie

Where-ivver ye gan, yor sure to find a Geordie
Where-ivver ye gan ye'll hear the Geordie twang
From Land's End up to John O' Groats
From Galway Bay to Cullercoats
Yor sure to meet a Geordie in the thrang
If ivver you tyek a trip someday to London
Ye needn't wear a lost and lonely air
Sing Blaydon Races doon the Strand
And somebody's sure to wag yor hand
Where-ivver you go a Geordie will be there

Where-ivver ye gan, yor sure to find a Geordie
Where-ivver ye gan yor native tongue you'll hear
In ivvery place across the sea
It myeks nee odds where it might be
Yor sure to hear a Geordie say 'Wot cheor'
From canny Newcastle, S*nd*rl*nd and Gateshead

From Tyne and Wear ye'll meet them ivvery where
There isn't a spot that ye can nyem
But somebody wants the news from hyem
Where-ivver ye gan a Geordie will be there

Where-ivver ye gan yor sure to find a Geordie
They're scattered aboot in regions het and caad
And ye can bet a silver croon
When rockets land upon the moon
There'll be a Geordie yellin' 'Keep ahaad'
So here is a song me canny lads to cheer ye
For after aall, this comfort ye can share
That when yor earthly days are past
Ye've got to leave this world at last
Where-ivver ye gan a Geordie will be there

And a bonus verse from the show transmitted on Guy Fawkes night...

Where-ivver ye gan yor sure to find a Geordie
To celebrate Guy Fawkes' night in style
For ammunition they have stacks
Of rockets, crackers, jumpy jacks
And ivverythin' that myeks the neet worthwhile
There'll be a greet big fire where folks are starin'
At Guy Fawkes sittin' in his brokken chair
Till up he shoots amang the stars
And heor some singin' up at Mars
Where-ivver ye gan a Geordie will be there

By Jack Robson
1885 - 1957

Keep't Dark

Aad Mistress Clark wes fond of a clash
She like'd to hear hor tongue
She said that taalkin' eased the mind
Wi' folks byeth aad an' young
The chep that knaas nowt's gud advice
Wes lost on Mistress Clark
But mind aa shuddn't menshun this
Aa hope ye'll aall keep't dark!

Says Mistress Clark to sevral friends
She had one day to tea,
Aa wonder what meks Geordie Haall
Se fond o' beer an' sprees?
The' say his wife can tek hor gill,
An' neether's fond o' wark,
But mind aa shuddn't menshun this,
Aa hope ye'll aall keep't dark!

There's Mary Smith upon the stairs
A wild an' rakish lass
Aa wunder where she gets hor claes
Aa's sure she has nee brass
They say she's thick wi' Draper Jim
He's not up tiv the mark
But mind aa shuddn't menshun this
Aa hope ye'll aall keep't dark!

There's Bella Jones that lives next door
Got Bessie Thompson's shaawl
An borra'd Suzy Ratcliffe's goon
To gan tiv Hopper's baall

But neether of' 'em's got 'em back
Aa think 'tis owt but a lark
But mind aa shuddn't menshun this,
Aa hope ye'll aall keep't dark!

There's Dolly Green that dorty slut
That lives alaang the yard
She florts wi' ivry lad she meets
She's worthy nee regard
Last neet aa catch'd her on the stairs
Wi' Jack the quayside clerk
But mind aa shuddn't menshun this
Aa hope ye'll aall keep't dark!

There's Mistress Johnson paans her claes
As sure as Monday comes
An' drunken Mary locks the door
For fear she'll get the bums
An' Mistress Black'll nivvor wesh
Her man a shart for wark
But mind aw shuddn't menshun this
Aa hope ye'll aall keep't dark!

Fat Mistress Jackson likes to clash
Lang Jinnie likes hor ways
An' Mary Riley starves hor bairns
To get sic dandy claes
Young Peggy Robson's got her bed
Throo sum seducin' spark
But mind aa shuddn't menshun this
Aa hope ye'll aall keep't dark!

By Joe Wilson

The Row Upon The Stairs

Says Mistress Bell to Mistress Todd
'Ye'd better clean the stairs!
Ye've miss'd yer torn for monny a week
the neybors aall did theirs!'
Sez Mistress Todd to Mistress Bell
'Aa tell ye, Mistress Bell
Ye'd better mind yer aan affairs
an' clean the stairs yorsel'

O what tongues i' the row upon the stairs
Clitterin, clatterin, scandal an' clash
I' the row upon the stairs

Sez Mistress Todd 'When it suits me
to think that it's me torn
Ye've a vast o' cheek to order me,
thor's not a wummin born
That keeps a cleaner hoose than me
an' mark ye, Mistress Bell
If ye'd owenly dee the syem as me
ye'd gan an' clean yersel!'

Says Mistress Bell 'Ye clarty fah,
whe was't that stole the beef?'
'What did ye say?' cries Mistress Todd,
'D'ye mean that aa'm a thief?
Let's hev the sixpence that aa lent
to treat Meg Smith wi' gin!
An' where's the blanket that ye got
the last time ye lay in?'

Says Mistress Bell 'Ye knaa yersel
the sixpence's lang been paid
An' that raggy blanket that ye lent
was nee use then, ye said!'
'A raggy blanket, Mistress Bell?'
cries Mistress Todd 'Whaat cheek!
Yor dorty stockin' had two holes
full twice the size last week!'

'Maa holey stockin's, Mistress Todd,
looks better in the street
Than your gud man's aad Blucher byuts
ye wear to hide yer feet!
The eer-rings ye got off the Jew
on tick the tother day
Will be like the fine manage man's shaawl
th' syem as gi'en away!'

Says Mistress Todd 'Ye geet skyet gob
ye'd bettor haad yor jaaw
The varry shift upon yor back
belangs the wife belaah!'
'Ye lazy wretch!' shoots Mistress Bell
it's true there is nee doot
Last neet ye fuddled wi' Bob the Snob
The time yer man wes oot!'

'Oh, Mistress Bell!' says Mistress Todd
'Ye brazend-luckin' slut
Ye may taawk away to clean the stairs
aa'll nivvor stor a fut!
Afore aa'd lift a scoorin' cloot
the mucky stairs to clean
Aa'd see them torn as black as ye
ye paanshop-luckin' queen!'

by Joe Wilson

The Hedgehog Pie

Aa'll sing ye a song if ye'll patiently wait
Aboot a grand supper there's been at Street Gate
Te eat this grand supper there only was two
But they ett a whole hedgehog, some bacon an' coo

chorus:
Singin' fal de ral laddy, sing fal de ral day
Fal de ral laddy, sing fal de ral day

There's a chap in the neyborhood has a smaall dog
One day went out waakin' an' it catched a hedgehog
So to hev a bit fun with the prize that they'd got
He thowt tiv hissel he wad tek it to Stott

When he took it to Stott they arranged what to dee
With Kingey an' Barbor they aalways made free
Every time they went there they were hungry an' dry
So just for the lark they wad mek them a pie

Nuw it had to be killed before startin' to skin't
So they took up a mell for to knock oot its wind
Them that was present th' roared an' th' laffed
The chep missed the hedgehog an' he brock the mell-shaft

The mell was nee use so they took a sharp knife
Detarmined to tek away Proggley's life
They tried for to kill him in two diff'rent ways
So they had to droon him for to finish his days

The landlady's sister made up a pie-crust
With the best o' beef-fat an' some dumplin' dust
She nicked it all roond, made it tender, an' then
The oven was hot, so she put the pie in

Nuw, Barbor an' Kingey sat winkin' their eye
Soon wishin' they ownly could get a bit pie
They were watchin' the mistress instead of their gill
The smell was that nice they could hardly keep still

Tom the butcher to suit them, soon found oot a plan
He sez, 'Drink off yor gills, be as sharp as ye can
Gan into the meat-hoose, an' let all things by
And aa'll watch the mistress an' steal ye the pie'

In the meat-hoose they ownly had been a short while
When they saa the pie comin', an' they started to smile
Tom says, 'Get it eaten 'twas fettled for Stott
If he comes he'll gan mad' Kingey says, 'Man, it's hot!'

Nuw to get the pie eaten they both wired in
Till the gravy ran off both their noses an' chin
When Stott showed the skin off the pie that they had
They' looked at each other, an' torned varry bad

Sez Barbor to Kingey 'Jack, aa wadn't care
But proggles come nuw where there used to be hair!
Aa bowt a hard hat, an' aa've tied it tight doon
But the proggles come faster, an' the've went through the croon'

A razor's no use, th' both shave with a saa
Like icicles faallin', they drop from their jaa
Barbor's in trouble an' Kingey far warse
He cannot lie down, or sit on his arse

By Tommy Armstrong

The Neybors Doon Belaa

Aa'll tell ye the dein's o' some o' the folks
That lives in wor neyborhood
Thor a lot o' lazy good for nowts
An' the myest o' them's far from good
From Sunday morn till Sat'day neet, thor cadgin' neet an' day
An' whativvor they borrow they nivvor retorn
So ye might as well hoy it away

They'll borrow yer onions, leeks an' peas
Whenivvor th' pot's to boil
They'll ask for a happ'ny candle if they canna get paraffin oil
Whativvor they borrow they nivvor retorn
Such folks aa nivvor saa
They'd skin a rat for its hide an' fat. The neybors doon belaa

Thor's Mistress Jones set up hor gob
An' axed iz what aa meant
'Cos aa wadd'nt lend hor haaf-a-croon
To help hor to pay the rent
Aa've lent hor money once afore but aa'll nivver dee't agyen
For she caalled iz a hot-heeded fiery feul
An' she hit iz wiv a styen

Aa started a shop, but oh! dear me, of that aa seun got sick
It wes like a clock that wadd'nt gan wivoot its favourite tick
The mainspring brock, the clock was then
Hoyed oot intiv the street
Aa often said that clock wad gan
If the neybors wad de reet

by James Weams

Wor Nanny's a Mazer

Wor Nanny an' me myed up wor minds to gan an' catch the train
Te gan t' the toon t' buy some claes for wor little Billy and Jane
But when we got to Rowland's Gill the mornin' train was gone
Tha wasn't another un gan' that way till siventeen minutes t'one
So aa sez t' wor Nan, 'It's a lang way t' gan'
Aa cud see biv hor fyece she wes vexed
But aa sez 'Nivvor mind. We hev plenty o' time
We'll stop an' we'll gan wi' the next'
She give a bit smile then aa spok up an sez,
'There's a pubberlick hoose alang heor
We'll gan alang there an' git worsels warm
An' a glass o' the best bittor beer'
But Nan wes see stoot aa knew she'd not waak
An she didn't seem willin' to try
When a think o' the trouble aa'd wi' hor that day
Aa's likely te borst oot an' cry

Chorus
And eeh wor Nanny's a mazer an' a mazer she'll remain
As lang as aa live aall nivvor forget the day we lost the train

So doon we went to the pubberlick hoose
An when we got to the door
She sez 'We'll gan intiv the parlour end
For aa've nivver been heor afore'
So in we went an' took wor seats
An' afore aa rang the bell
Aa axed hor what she was gannin' te hev
And she sez, 'The syem as yorsel'
So aa caalled for two gills of the best bittor beer
She paid for them when they come in

An afore she'd swallied a haaf o' hors
She said 'Aa wad rather hev gin'
So aa caalled for a glass o' the best Hollands Gin
She swallied it doon the forst try
Aa sez to wor Nan 'Thoo's as good as a man'
She sez 'Bob, man, aa feel varry dry'

She sat an' drank till she got tight
She sez 'Bob, man. Aa feel varry queer'
Aa sez, 'Thoo's had nine glasses o' gin
to my two gill's o' beer'
She lowsed hor hat an' then hor shaawl
An' hoyed them on the floor
Aa thowt wor Nan was gan' wrang iv hor mind
So aa sat mesel next tiv the door
She sez 'Give iz order. Aa'll sing a bit sang'
Aa sat an aa glowered at hor
Aa thowt she wes jokin' for aa nivvor hord
Wor Nanny sing ony afore
She tried te stand up te sing the Cat Pie
But she fell doon an' myed sic a clatter
She smashed fower chairs, an' the Landlord come in
An' he sez 'What the deuce is the matter?'

He sez te me 'Is this yer wife?
An' where de ye belang?'
Aa sez 'It is, an' she's tyun a fit
Wi tryin' te sing a bit sang'
He flung his arms aroond hor waist
And trailed hor ower the floor
An' poor aad Nan (like a dorty hoose cat)
Was hoyed oot side o' the door
An' there she wes lyin', both groanin' an cryin'

Te claim hor aa really thowt shyem
Aa tried to lift hor, but aa cudn't shift hor
An' aa wished aa had Nanny at hyem
The paper man said he wad give hor a lift
So we hoisted hor intiv the trap

But Nan was that tight that she cudn't sit up
So wuz fasten'd hor down wiv a strap
She cuddn't sit up and she waddn't lie doon
An' she kicked till she brock the conveyance
She lost a new basket, hor hat an hor shaawl
That woman, wi lossin' the trains

By Tommy Armstrong

Cushy Butterfield

Aa's a brokken hearted keelman an' aa's owerheed in love
Wiv a young lass from Gatesheed an' aa caalls hor my dove
Hor name's Cushie Butterfield and she sells yeller clay
An' hor cousin is a muckman an' they caall him Tom Grey

She's a big lass an' a bonny lass
An' she likes hor beer
An' they call hor Cushie Butterfield
An aa wish she was here

Her eyes is like two holes in a blanket bornt through
An her brows of a mornin' would spyen a young coo
An' when aa hears hor shoutin' 'Will you buy any clay?'
Like a candyman's trumpet she steals me poor heart away

Ye'll oft see 'er doon at Sandgit when the fresh herrin comes in
She's like a bagful of saawdust tied roond iv a bit string
She wears big galoshes too an hor stockin's once was white
And her bed-goon is lilac an hor hat's nivvor strite

When I axed hor t' marry iz she started t' laugh.
She sez 'Nen o' yer monkey tricks cos aa'll hev nee such chaff'
Then she started a bubblin' an' she roared like a bull
An' the cheps on the keel sez aa's nowt but a fyul

She sez 'The chep that gets iz'll hev t' work every day
An' when he comes hyem at neet he'll hev t' gan an' seek clay
An' while he's away seekin' it aa'll mek balls and sing
Oh, weel may the keel row that my laddie's in'

By George Ridley

The Day We Went T' The Coast

By Johnny Handle

Here's one of my favourite Geordie songs. It was written in the sixties by Johnny Handle and passed on through the folk clubs. This is the way I learned it. I hope it's not too far from the original.

There's songs that's sung aboot the pits
There's songs aboot the sea
Nuw here's a topical kind of song, aa think ye will agree
It's aall aboot wor Aggie and hor man that she caalls Joe
And aall the folks alang wor street, wuz tiv the coast did go

Wey the day was fine when we set off to get the 'lectric train
Aah thowt, now John, tek alang yer cap
Cos ye knaa that it might rain
Wey we bundled aall the kids an' aall and mind there was a few
The checky waved his flag aboot and then the whistle blew

There was Ma and Pa and owld Granda
And the bloke that lived nextdoor
He had to fetch his lodger alang and he browt a canny few more
There was Aggie and Bert and Bella and Alf
and aall their bits o' bairns
The cackle fleeing on the train was like ten thousand hens

Nuw nee sooner had we got to the coast and aa was settled doon
The bairns was rushing for ice cream
shootin 'Lend us haff a croon'
Aa licked me lips, me jaaws was dry, aa sez 'That's just the job'
But aa got more ice cream aall ower me shart
than ivver went in me gob

Nuw later on aa settled doon to sleep upon the sand
Aa hord a soond aal pitter poond, so I held oot both me hands
Wey, hell, ye can guess, it started to rain,
ye've nivvor seen such fun
As aall the folks alang wor street for shelter they did run

There was fowerty thoosand on wuz there,
aall packed intiv the shelter
We was eatin wor bait and enjoyin worsels,
the rain did soak and pelter
Aa reached intiv me pocket for to grab mesel a bite
And this geet big lad aside us sez 'Huw kid, d'ye want a fight?'

'Aall borst yer fyess,' he sez to me 'For howkin aboot like that'
So aa dropped mesel doon on aall fours afore aa copped a bat
The fists and bottles sharp did flee and as aa craawled away
There was fowerty pollises came alang to join in wi' the fray

Wey soon it was time for us to gan, aall on we that wuz gannin
There was fowerty thoosand on the train,
nee room for nowt but stannin'
Wuz wor gan' through Waalker station,
up speaks me owld grandad
Sayin' 'John, where is yer father? Cos wuz cannot find the lad'

So we coonted aall assembled there. Me da could not be seen
Then up speaks little Jimmy, sayin 'Aa knaa where he has been,
Ye mind when we was digging sand and howkin aall aboot?
Wey we buried me father in the sand and forgot to dig 'im oot!'

Noo aa mind the Blaydon Races, aa mind Nan o' Rowlands Gill
And aa mind stottin' alang the wall when aa hev had a gill
Aa mind the day that aa got wed but the day aa mind the most
Was the day me fatha skelpt me arse for buryin' 'im at th' coast!

Adopted Geordies

Over the years sportsmen and celebrities have found a place in the hearts of Tyneside folks and if it was possible we would bestow upon them an honorary Geordieship. Strangely, not all Newcastle footballers have made it on to the list. Perhaps it's something to do with their attitude whilst playing or after leaving the club. Who knows?

Kevin Keegan, Pavel Srnicek, Shay Given, Nolberto Solano,
Phillipe Albert, Rob Lee, George & Ted Robledo,
Malcolm MacDonald, Bobby Robson, Pop Robson,
John Beresford, John Anderson, Les Ferdinand,
Bobby Moncur, Shola Ameobi, Glen Roeder, Gary Speed,
Wyn Davies, Hughie Gallagher,
Jonothan Edwards - Athlete, Mark & Dave Knopfler,
Johnny Wilkinson - Newcastle and England rugby player,
Simon Newell - The 'Geordie' from Alan Partridge,
Tanni Grey Thompson - Great North Run,
Basil Mott & David Hay built the Tyne Bridge,
Isaac Guillory - Virtuoso guitarist,
Jeremiah Dixon - Surveyor/Astronomer,
Emperor Hadrian, St Aiden, St Cuthbert, Robert Curthose,
Chano, Eddy and Chico from Apu - Traditional Peruvian band,
James Bolam and Rodney Bewes - for the Likely Lads,
Charles Parsons - Engineer,
Dick Clement - Writer, Anna Friel - In the film Goal,
Catherine Tate for 'Georgie', Gilbert the Alien (Phil Cornwell)
Enrique's mole - Leigh Francis,
Harry Enfield -'Nar, it's gone,'
Paul Whitehouse - Hulio Geordio,
Two of the Baghdaddies Band,
Toon supporters: Norman Wisdom, Tony Blair, Basil Hume.
As we go to press Michael Owen has only played played eleven games so still has to earn the honour.

Dave the Jackal

From 'More *Fairly* Truthful Tales'

Come an' listen to me an' I'll tell yuz a tale
That you might or you might not believe
Of a weird and wonderful occurrence
What some folks'll find hard to porceive

Now I knaa the majority of folks rund these parts
Can manage from cradle to grave
Havin' sod aall to dee wi' a jackal as such
But this tale's aboot one, - caalled Dave

Nuw jackals, ye knaa, accordin' to me da
Are wild dogs wi' geet sticky-up ears
That live where it's hot, - deserts and whatnot
So you'll not see that many rund here

He lived on the ootskorts of Cape Toon, did Dave
In Sooth Africa an' 'e thowt THAT was dull
That's till he went scroongin' in a truck full of apples
An' ended up in a warehoose in Hull

Dis-orient-icated, I think, is the word
After six thoosand miles in a crate
And it took a few weeks wi' just apples to eat
So 'is bowels warn't behavin' too great

Then they set off again wi' him still in 'is box
But he'd chowed through the top and was hidin'
In the hope that he'd be in The Serengetee
But he wasn't. It was Plodgeborough Sidin's

When there was nee one aboot, he got heself oot
Had a stretch and a bloody good scratch
And set off across Plodgeborough Common
To find a wildebeest or summat to catch

There was nowt but a hedgehog and he couldn't eat that
Then he wound up in Gudgeon's scrap yard
Where he comes nose-to-nose wi' a rottweiler caalled Rose
And he thowt 'Flippin heck! She looks hard!'

The rottweiler was nice but, she stopped and thowt twice
Aboot swallyin' wor poor Dave whole
She says 'Aalreet there, my love?' then says 'Heavens above,
You need a good feed. Where's me bowl?'

She says 'Here, have some dinner, 'fore you get any thinner,
I could play 'Owld Lang Syne' on yer ribcage'
She says 'I like skinny blokes but yer havin' a joke,
Think you'd nivver been fed since the Ice age'

With the flame from the Plodgeborough Cokeworks
Reflectin' in the pond underneath
She looked quite attractive stood there in the dusk
Wi' a sparkle tiv her eyes and hor teeth

She invited Dave to stay at hor place that neet
A blue Bedford van she caalled home
And the two of 'em got geet nice and cosy
As snug as two lops in a comb

Nuw while Rose was quite happy confined tiv her yard
Wor Dave was more programmed to roam
An' gan huntin' for prey, so as he went oot next day
Sayin' 'Divvent cook owt. I'll bring summat home'

There's not much caall for a Jackal in Plodgeborough but
There's nee gazelles, nee wilderbeest n'that
Nee wide desert plains and nee pampas nor nowt
'Less you coont the spare field by wor flats

It was Plodgeborough High Street where Dave ended up
Where the butcher was unloadin' 'is van
So Dave went to grund till he wasn't arund
Then lowped in an' done off with a ham

Nuw Rose was that used to eatin' Pedigree Chum
She didn't take kindly to change
So bein' polite she just buried it that night
And Dave din't think anythin' strange

So once they'd got used tiv each other's strange ways
And adapted their lifestyle to suit
They lived oot their life like husband and wife
And had three lots of puppies to boot

It's sad, I suppose, that poor Dave and Rose
Passed on many years ago now
And though they've long gone, their legend lives on
If you listen I'll tell you for how

You see aall dogs in toon, be they collies or poms
Chihuahuas, alsations or pugs
They've all got that sparkle in their eyes and their teeth
And they've all got geet sticky-up lugs!

Geordie Phobias

(As published in the Chance't)

Fear of bees – Bummlerphobia

Fear of birds – Spuggyphobia

Fear of closing time – Nighonlowseaphobia

Fear of speed – Tappylappaphobia

Fear of losing to S*nd*rl*nd – Pisstekaphobia

DIVVENT BE SOFT, MAN WOMAN!

YER NOT SCARED OF A MOOSE!

Fear of being below S*nd*rl*nd in the league
Yermockinbutaphobia

Fear of girls – Tottaphobia

Fear of Christmas shopping – Fenwickaphobia

Fear of seafood – Willockaphobia

Fear of germs – Lurgysmittaphobia

Fear of Man Utd scoring in extra time –
Jammynowtsaphobia

Fear of paying bills – Provvyblokeaphobia

Fear of mediocrity – Nowtstartlinaphobia

Fear of getting lost on Wearside –
Notbloodypenshermonumentagainaphobia

Fear of open spaces – Ootbyeaphobia

HUW LANG SINCE YE'VE BEEN OOT?

175

Temperature Explained

There have been versions of this doing the rounds for years.
It has been adapted by folks from Inverness to Minnesota.
Here's the Geordie version:

50 degrees Fahrenheit – People in southern England decide it's time to turn on their central heating. Argos in Newcastle have run out of desk fans and beer coolers.

40 degrees – Southerners shiver indoors while Geordies pack the beach at Cullercoats.

35 degrees – The AA is overwhelmed by cars in the south of England refusing to start. People in Newcastle and Gateshead are driving with their sunroofs open and windows down.

20 degrees – Southerners wear overcoats, gloves and woolly hats. Geordies might throw on a T-shirt.

15 degrees – Southerners begin to evacuate to the equator while people from Newcastle swim in the North Sea at Amble.

Zero degrees – London grinds to a halt. Geordies have their last barbecue before it gets cold.

Minus 10 degrees – Life in the south has ceased to exist. Newcastle folk have to buy jackets.

Minus 80 degrees – Polar bears wonder if it's worth carrying on. Boy Scouts in Newcastle start wearing their long trousers.

Minus 100 degrees – Santa Claus abandons North Pole. There's a rush on vests and long johns at M&S Metro Centre.

SO WHY ARE WE TWINNIN TOWNS
WITH WALBOTTLE?

Minus 173 degrees – Alcohol freezes. Geordies riot as pubs are forced to close.

Minus 297 degrees – Microbial life starts to disappear. Cows on the Town Moor complain about farmers with cold hands

Minus 460 degrees – All atomic motion stops and Newcastle folk are forced to stamp their feet and blow on their hands

Minus 500 degrees – Hell freezes over. S*nd*rl*nd qualify for Europe.

Glossary

A'cos - Because
A'haad - A hold
A'hint - Behind
Aa - I
Aa'll - I will
Aad - Old
Aall - all
Aalreet - Allright
Aan - Own
Aboot - About
Afore - Before
Alang - Along
Alairn - Alone
Any amoont - Plenty
Anyhoo/Anyhuw - Anyway
Aye - Yes
Bairn - Child
Bait - Food
Balmbra's - A music hall in Newcastle
Bint - Girl, girlfriend
Bleezer - Blazer (Metal sheet to aid draught when firelighting)
Blethor - Gossip
Bonna - Bonfire
Bonny - Nice, Pleasant or Pretty
Boozah - Inn or Public house
Born - Stream or Burn
Borst - Burst (See chin)
Bowk - Throw up
Bowt - Bought
Brahma - Excellent
Brokken - Broken
Broon - Brown
Broon Dog - Newcastle Brown Ale
Bubble - Cry
Bullets - Sweets

Caad - Cold
Canny - Good, nice, really
Cack - Horsemuck
Chaalk - Chalk
Champion - Great
Chep - Old man
Chin - Beat up, attack
Chowa - Chewing gum
Chuffed - Pleased
Clag - Sticky
Clart - Mud
Clock - Look at
Club - Credit account
Coin - Turn
Cowld - Cold
Cowp - Fall
Coyboys - Cowboys
Crack - Chat
Crackett - A stool, box, or chest for sitting on
Cuddy - A cow or a horse
Da - Father
Darza - Lovely, impressive
Dee - Do
Deed - Dead
Dicky - Flea, headlice
Divvent/Divvint - Do not
Dog - Newcastle Brown Ale
Dorty - Dirty
Dyke - Wall or hedgerow
Eez - His or he has
Ett - Eaten, Ate
Fettle - Condition or fix or break!
Flannins - Flannels or long-johns
Forgettn - Forgot
Fower pennorth - portion of chips

Fyece - Face
Gaawk - Stare
Gadgy - Man
Gallowa - Cart horse
Gan - Go
Gannie/ganny - Grandmother
Gannin' or gan' - Going
Ganzie - Sweater/pullover
Gettn' - Getting or Got
Givower - Desist
Greggs Dummy - Sausage roll
Gyetsid - Gateshead
Haad - Hold
Hacky - Dirty
Hadaway - Go away
Heed - Head
Heed-the-baall - Idiot
Heor - Hear or here
Hev - Have
Hinny - Affectionate term for friend, partner, lover (male or female)
Hintend - Back end, bottom
Hitchy Dabbas - Hopscotch
Hoose - House
Hoppins - Fair
Howkin - Picking or Punching
Howway - Come on, Come here
Hoy - Throw   On the hoy - Drinking
Hyem - Home
Ivvry - Every
Iz - Me
Jarra - Jarrow
Keks -Trousers
Kittled - Tickled
Knaa - Know
Knaan - Known
Knacked - Hurt
Larn - Learn or teach
Laggyband - Elastic band

Lowse - Home time
Mackem - Inhabitant of S*nd*rl*nd
Ma - Mother
Manors - Station, not quite city centre
Marra - Friend
Me - My
Meggin - Lying, Telling untruths
Mek - Make
Mell - Hammer
Mesel - Myself
Monkeyhanger - Inhabitant of Hartlepool
Mortal - Very drunk
Narf - Not half
Nee - No (None)
Netty - Lavatory
Nigh - Near
Nigh on - Almost
Nivvor - Never
Nuw/Noo - Now
Nowt - Nothing/unimportant person
Nowt startlin - Nothing special
Onaccoonter - As a result of
On't - On it or of it. Aa'm sick on't.
Oot - Out
Oppen - Open
Ower - Over, too
Owld - Old
Owt - Anything
Oxter - Armpit
Paanshop - Pawn shop
Pet - Affectionate term for friend of the opposite sex or woman to woman
Pinny - Apron
Pitmatic - Dialect of the north-east pit villages
Pittle - Urine/Urinate
Plodgin - Paddling
Plumb - Straight

Poke - Trouser pocket, bag or sack
Pollis - Policeman
Porpoise - Purpose
Prog - Poke
Pund - Pound
Pyet - Head
Reed Raa - The village of Red Row
Reet - Right
Rive - Rip
Roond - Round
RVI - Royal Victoria Infirmary
Sacatarry - Secretary
Sackless - Dopey, lazy
Sand dancer - Inhabitants of
South Shields
Santy - Santa Claus
Santy Pants - Red trousers
Scran - Food
Scranshuns - Scraps of batter
Sharp - Early, soon
Shin - Climb
Shuggy Boats - Fairground ride
Skeets - Boots
Skyet gob - Fish face
Smit - Infection
Smoggie - Inhabitant of Teesside
Snaa - Snow
Snadgy - Turnip
Sneck - Nose or doorlatch
Spelk - Splinter, small person
Squitts - Evens
Stott - Bounce
Stowed off - Crowded
Strang - Strong
Strides - Trousers
Strite - Straight
Summat/summick - Something
Tab - Cigarette
Tatie/Tettie - Potato

Tek - Take
Telt - Told
Tettie - Potato
Th' morn/ The morra - Tomorrow
Th' morns neet - Tomorrow night
Th'day - Today
Thowt - Thought
Tiddlers - Small fish
Tiv - To
Tyun - Taken
Varnigh - Very nearly
Wad - Would
Waddn't - Would not
Watter - Water
Whaddya - Would you/What do you
Whe - Who
Whisht! - Be quiet
Wey - Well
Wifey - Woman
Willock - Shellfish
Winnet -Will not
Woollyback - People from out of
Town
Wor - Our
Worky ticket - Troublemaker
Wrang - Wrong
Wuz - We
Yark - Hit, strike
Ye - You
Yu - You
Yer - You, Your or You're
Yersel - Yourself
Yon - That, There, Those
Young'un – Child, young brother
Yu - You
Yuz - You (Plural)

Quiz Answers

1   The Ministry of National Insurance then Ministry of Pensions and National Insurance.
2   Chimney Mill
3   Dene Motor Company
4   Ginger Beer
5   La Dolce Vita
6   The Tatler, Haymarket
7   Dame Flora Robson
8   Jesmond Vale
9   Gosforth High Street
10 The Regal
11 PJ and Duncan – Ant and Dec
12 Cheryl Tweedy –Girls Aloud
13 Neil Tennent – Pet Shop Boys
14 Michael Carrick
15 Barbecue Express
16 Barras Bridge
17 Brandling Park
18 The Central Library
19 Dan Smith
20 Alf Roberts
21 United
22 Heaton Secondary, later renamed Heaton Grammar then Heaton Manor
23 Caledonian Princess
24 Westgate Road
25 Andrews Liver Salts
26 Weighing 53 Stones, he was the heaviest man in Britain. The building was partially dismantled and a winch constructed to remove his body to a horse drawn lorry.
27 Parish's Department Store
28 Dr Gibbs
29 Bainbridge & Co
30 Ropemaker
31 Maling
32 He became an MP in 1874
33 Bernard Youens – Stan Ogden
34 Herby Ray's
35 Admiral Collingwood

36	The Swing Bridge joins the High Level Bridge
37	The Swing Bridge
38	The Town Hall
39	Westmorland Road / Cruddas Park
40	Joe Wilson
41	No. It was written as a broadsheet to sell at the race meeting and was first performed on the 5th of June 1862.
42	The Barry Sisters
43	Don Warrington
44	Grainger Market
45	The Assembly Rooms, Westgate Road
46	1854
47	The first steam turbine ship – The Turbinia
48	George and Ted Robledo
49	It was presented by a Prime Minister – Winston Churchill
50	Lancelot Capability Brown
51	Arsenal
52	Earl Grey. The monument was struck by lightning.
53	Hedley Chapman – Siesta House
54	George and Robert Stephenson
55	The Central Station
56	Dog racing
57	Haymarket
58	John Woodvine
59	Libby Davison
60	Charlie Hardwick
61	Robson Green
62	Denise Welch
63	Sammy Johnson
64	Peter Beardsley
65	Paul Gascoigne
66	Pavel Srnicek
67	Donna Air
68	Billy Fane
69	Jill Halfpenny
70	To stop transportation of coal during the General Strike of 1926, Cramlington miners removed part of the main rail track. Unfortunately, the first train through was The Flying Scotsman!
71	A pub on Scotswood Road
72	Glen McCrory
73	Princess Anne

74	Milk Market
75	George Stephenson
76	Jayne Middlemiss
77	Lawrie McMenemy
78	Jackie Milburn
79	Duran Duran
80	Blackett Street
81	Upper Dean Street
82	The first all-ticket match
83	The first penalty scored (Against Barnsley – in a replay)
84	The Mauretania
85	Blyth
86	The Metro Centre car park
87	Hawthorn Leslie, Armstrong Whitworth, Swan Hunter, Vickers Armstrong, Wigham Richardson.
88	The Shadows
89	Prelude
90	The Animals
91	Gallowgate Public Bath House
92	The Northumberland Arms
93	St James' Hall
94	The Grainger Market
95	Central Arcade
96	Central Station
97	The Sage, Gateshead
98	The Tyne Pedestrian Tunnel
99	Blackett Street
100	Grainger Street
101	Wenger's Department Store
102	Northumberland Street
103	Bigg Market
104	Sting
105	Brian Johnson
106	Jimmy Nail
107	Lindisfarne
108	Mark Knopfler
109	Thomas Pumphrey
110	It was Temperance festival set up to rival the Newcastle Races.
111	WD & HO Wills
112	The Newcastle Arena. Brainchild of Chas Chandler and Nigel Stanger
113	The Royalty

114	Jesmond Dene
115	Leazes Park
116	Paddy Freeman's
117	Nun's Moor Park
118	Jesmond Vale
119	Exhibition Park
120	Saltwell Park
121	St Thomas Street
122	Fossway
123	A bridge over the lake
124	Bath Lane
125	Hagg Bank, Wylam
126	Corbridge
127	Ovingham to Prudhoe
128	Newburn to Ryton
129	Rowing
130	Bobby Moncur
131	High Bridge
132	Groat Market
133	Cluny
134	Domestos
135	Britain's Friendliest City
136	The most beautiful street in Britain
137	The Ouseburn
138	Heaton – Stratford, Bolingbroke, Hotspur, etc.
139	It joins Forth Street with Neville Street
140	Skinnerburn Road
141	Darn Crook
142	He was hung
143	Nelson's Column, Trafalgar Square, London.
144	Brunswick
145	Rowan Atkinson
146	The Newcastle Hero
147	The Monkey Bar
148	73
149	The Civic Centre
150	The Victoria Tunnel

And Finally....

A lot has been said in this book about our proud heritage. The rich lands of the North East were fought over for centuries bringing bloodshed, misery and hardship to our people. Through hard work, belief and commitment, the Geordies survived.

Whilst sustaining the mining communities, the Great North Coalfield provided the wealth to make Newcastle a city of commerce and innovation. Coal was the fuel of the industrial revolution and provided the pioneers Stephenson, Parsons, Armstrong and many more, with the resources to lead the world with their inventions. Without coal, would Tyneside have had the factories, heavy engineering, iron, steel and shipbuilding? Would the Tyne have been one of the busiest rivers in Europe? Would Newcastle Gateshead be what it is today?

Our greatest debt must be to the humble miner. Men and boys often paid with their lives – either in the many pit disasters and accidents or through longer term health problems. Malcolm Collins wrote this heart-rending song:

Martha's Lament

Chorus
'Howway, Son. How Geordie, come cuddle up close,
The bairns, they'll aall miss ye, aye lad, aa'll miss ye most,
Howway, Son. How Geordie, come haad us up tight,
Aall put me arms roond ye, aa'll kiss ye goodnight'

'Aye Geordie, d'ye mind the day we wor wed?
The ale that was drunk and the tears that wor shed?
Me own bonny pit lad, se fine and se young,
Before aall that coaldust had clogged up yer lungs'

'Aye, Geordie,' thowt Martha, as she held his frail frame
'How many more lads will that dorty pit claim?
How many young pitmen, diggin' for coal,
Are ganna pay with their lives or they'll pay with their souls?'

And Geordie hord Martha, as she gave a sigh
She was howldin' back tears as they brimmed in hor eyes
She thowt of the happy years, how they had fled
As the moon cast gaunt shadders from that grimy pithead

So why must a man work doon that black hole?
Why must he breath lungs full of dust from the coal?
So shovel yer coal on but spare time to pray
For the man who works where there is no night or day

Aye, and spare thowt for Martha and her little bairns
Spare thowt for Geordie, how he met his end
Think aboot Lofthouse, the miners who died
Tell me do ye still like that flickerin fireside?

Martha held Geordie close tiv hor breast
Geordie he struggled for his final breath
Geordie passed on. She held him tight
And for the very last time, Martha kissed him goodnight

Other titles written by Gary Hogg:

A Fistful of Pickles
Fairly Truthful Tales
More Fairly Truthful Tales
Fairly Truthful Tales CD
Amblethwaite 'Appenings CD

A selection of titles illustrated by Gary Hogg:

Shorts For All Occasions
Comedy by Bernard Wrigley

Ghostly Tales of Northumbria
Childrens book by Davydd Chong

The Student Handbook for Drama Series
By Brian McGuire

Suggested reading:
Todd's Geordie Words and Phrases - Todd
A Dictionary of North East Dialect - Bill Griffiths
Geordies; Roots of Regionalism - Colls & Lancaster
Quays to Newcastle - Quickfall
A Fine And Private Place - Morgan
Larn Yersel Geordie - Dobson

Websites worth a visit:
www.garyhogg.co.uk
www.northern-heritage.co.uk
www.geordie.co.uk
www.nufc.com
www.monkchester.co.uk
www.newcastleupontynedailyphoto.com
www.fredhogg.co.uk
www.bernardwrigley.com